The Great American Guest House Book

(Bed & Breakfast)

THE GREAT AMERICAN GUEST HOUSE BOOK

John Thaxton

1982/83

BURT FRANKLIN & CO.

Published by Burt Franklin & Company, Inc.
235 East Forty-fourth Street
New York, New York 10017

Manufactured in the United States of America

1 3 4 2

CONTENTS

INTRODUCTION

Experience people as well as places, pamper yourself, save money, look at Manhattan from a terrace high above, sleep in a lighthouse, on a houseboat, in a beautifully restored mansion listed in the National Register of Historic Places—these are just a few of the things I hope this book will help its readers enjoy. *The Great American Guest House Book* is the book smart travelers have been waiting for. It is the most comprehensive guide to one of the more comfortable and least costly forms of lodging: bed and breakfast. What has long been an English and European tradition seems almost overnight to have caught on in North America in a big way. This book is meant to help you learn how it works and how to make it work for you.

Guest houses vary tremendously, but the owners of nearly all share a desire to provide visitors with something special, with a form of lodging that's as old as it is new—spending the night in someone's home. Before World War II, guest houses, then frequently called "tourist homes," existed throughout the country as the principal lower-cost alternative to hotels along America's highways. Many of these guest houses have survived and are experiencing a resurgence in popularity, again as a lower-cost alternative to the high cost of hotels and the sterility of motels. Many guest houses are themselves historic buildings or were recently converted from historic structures; others are in popular locations near the mountains or seashore. During the past several years, thousands of Americans have opened their homes to guests while others have acquired and renovated homes far larger than they need with the express purpose of taking in guests. Recently bed-and-breakfast organizations—each of which acts as an agent for a number of guest houses, serving as a clearing house between guests and hosts—have sprung up in such places as Chicago, New York, San Francisco, the Napa Valley in California, Boston, the Hamptons on Long Island, Cape Cod in Massachusetts, Washington, D.C., and Vancouver, Montreal, and Toronto in Canada, to name just a few.

How to Use This Book

The guest houses described in this book fall into two broad categories—those you contact directly and those that accept reservations only through a referral service. As the bed-and-breakfast movement is new, the various referral services operate differently: Some require small membership fees, and others do not; some focus on a particular area or city, others cover the entire country; some collect fees for the host homes, others do not. The directors of the bed-and-breakfast referral services tend to be as friendly as the hosts they represent, and a brief phone call or letter will clarify exactly how a particular service currently operates.

In this book the guest houses that are represented by a referral service are briefly described, and each description is followed by the name and telephone number of the organization that should be contacted. Below is a listing—with names, addresses, and telephone numbers—of all the bed-and-breakfast referral services mentioned in this volume.

The other type of accommodation represented in this book is more after the fashion of a small inn. Entries describing this type tend to be longer, and specific details are provided, including information on facilities for children and pets, driving instructions, and mention of such amenities as air conditioning and television.

Most of the referral services have many additional listings, and their staffs will be happy to help you find just the location you are looking for. When contacting these services, try to be as specific as possible about your requirements: If you will be traveling with children, be sure to mention that. If you will be traveling on business and may need the use of a private telephone or parking facilities, remember to make that clear. If you will need to be in a downtown location close to public transportation, be sure to state that. If you'll be on vacation and would like access to a swimming pool, the beach, tennis courts, or a golf course, be sure to request those amenities. If you'll be bringing along the family dog and want a home that accepts pets or is near a kennel, most referral services will make an effort to fill that need. This book offers access to a very wide range of lodgings. Again if you're clear and specific about your needs, you'll be likely to find just what you're looking for.

This book has been organized alphabetically by state or Canadian province and, within each state or province, alphabetically by city or town. Individually described guest houses follow those accommodations available through referral services in the same town.

Rates

Rates for those accommodations available through referral services have been listed at the end of each entry. Rates for guest houses you can contact directly have been listed in the Index, along with credit-card information. Rates vary widely, based on the number of persons sharing accommodations and on the particular season of travel. Holiday periods are generally more expensive. Be sure to confirm the rate you will be paying when making reservations.

A Word of Advice

Making a reservation at a bed-and-breakfast place is not like making a reservation at a motel, where you can call at any hour of the night or day and usually find a room available. Unlike a motel, where you can pull in at any hour and get a soft drink from a machine, a guest house tends to be more like someone's home. Most people who have opened their homes to guests are warm and friendly and will go out of their way to make you feel comfortable, but they cannot be expected to provide the services of a large hotel with bellhops, bartenders, and waiters. On the other hand, expect the unexpected: perhaps afternoon tea with your host's personal friends, sherry served on the porch upon your arrival, fresh flowers in your bedroom, or a hostess willing to baby-sit while you're off exploring the village. Be sure that your children or pets behave appropriately, and I am sure you will have fun and a pleasurable trip.

If you plan to stay at a guest house, you should make reservations as early as possible. If it's not their busy season, hosts may not be home the first time you call them, and referral services tend to operate only during regular business hours in their local time zones.

I hope my readers have as much fun meeting new people and staying in new places as I have. Since I plan to revise and update this book on a regular basis, I would like to hear from readers. A reader's report is printed on the last page of this book. I look forward to receiving your comments, suggestions, and recommendations of guest houses you believe might merit inclusion in future editions.

JOHN THAXTON

Bed-and-Breakfast Reservation Services

Please note: Some reservation services charge a small membership fee; others do not. Most will supply a complete list of their accommodations to those sending a self-addressed, stamped envelope. Several require a small fee to cover the cost of mailing expenses. Contact the individual services, as listed below, for specific requirements.

Alberta Bed and Breakfast, 1330 Eighth Street SW #750, Calgary, Alberta T2R 1B6, Canada, (403) 233-8148; or 4327 Eighty-sixth Street, Edmonton, Alberta Y6K 1A9, Canada, (403) 462-8885.

American Bed and Breakfast Program, P.O. Box 983, St. Albans, VT 05478, (802) 524-4731, Bob Precoda. Vermont guest houses with asterisks after their names are members of this program.

The B & B Group (New Yorkers at Home), 301 East Sixtieth Street, New York, NY 10022, (212) 838-7015, Farla Zammit.

Bed and Breakfast Atlanta, 1221 Fairview Road NE, Atlanta, GA 30306, (404) 378-6026, Madalyne Eplan.

Bed and Breakfast Birmingham, P.O. Box 31328, Birmingham, AL 35222, (205) 591-6406, Ruth Taylor.

Bed and Breakfast Chicago, 1316 Judson Avenue, Evanston, IL 60201, (312) 328-8966, Janet Remen and Tommy Solberg.

Bed and Breakfast Colorado, P.O. Box 20596, Denver, CO 80220, (303) 333-3340, Rick Madden.

Bed and Breakfast Exchange, 1118 Pine Street, St. Helena, CA (707) 963-7127, Andee Beresini.

Bed and Breakfast Hawaii, P.O. Box 449, Kappa, Hawaii 96746, (808) 822-1582, Al Davis and Evelyn Warner.

Bed and Breakfast International, 151 Ardmore Road, Kensington, CA 94707, (415) 525-4569 or (415) 527-8836, Jean Brown.

The Bed and Breakfast League, 2855 Twenty-ninth Street NW, Washington, DC 20008, (202) 232-8718, Diana MacLeish.

Bed and Breakfast of Philadelphia, P.O. Box 101, Oreland, PA 19075, (215) 884-1084, Janet Mochel.

Bed and Breakfast of the Palm Beaches, 205 Circle West, Jupiter, FL 33458, (305) 746-2545, Eliza Hofmeister and Dolly Sherman.

Benson House of Richmond, P.O. Box 15131, Richmond, VA 23227, (804) 321-6277 or (804) 649-4601, Lyn Benson.

Country Host, R.R. 1, Palgrave, Ontario K2H 7T9, (519) 941-7633.

Guesthouses Bed and Breakfast, P.O. Box 5737, Charlottesville, VA 22903, (804) 973-7403, Sally Reger.

Hospitality Plus Bed and Breakfast, P.O. Box 1066, Scottsboro, AL 35768, (205) 259-1298, Norman and Jerry Brunton.

House Guests Cape Cod, 85 Hokum Rock Road, Dennis, MA 02638, (617) 385-8322, Allison Caswell.

The International Spareroom, Box 518, Solana Beach, CA 92075, (714) 755-3194 (until 11/6/82, thereafter (619) 755-3194), Muriel Foster.

Lodgings Plus Bed and Breakfast, P.O. Box 279, East Hampton, NY 11937, (516) 324-6740 or (212) 858-9589, Erwin Srob and Sara Flokos.

Montreal Bed and Breakfast, 4692 Kent Avenue, Montreal, Quebec H3W 1H1, Canada, (514) 738-3859, Marian Kahn.

Nashville Bed and Breakfast, P.O. Box 15651, Nashville, TN 37215, (615) 327-4546 or (615) 292-2574.

New England Bed and Breakfast, 1045 Centre Street, Newton, MA 02159, John Gardner.

Northwest Bed and Breakfast, 7707 SW Locust Street, Tigard, OR 97223, (503) 246-8366 or 246-2383, Laine Friedman and Gloria Shaich.

Suncoast Accommodations in Florida, P.O. Box 12, Palm Harbor, FL 33563, (813) 393-7020, Barbara Seligman.

Sweet Dreams and Toast, P.O. Box 4835-0035, Washington, DC, (202) 363-4712, Liz Cooke.

Toronto Bed and Breakfast, Box 86, Station T, Toronto, Ontario M6 3Z9, Canada, (416) 769-0612, Randy Lee.

Town and Country Bed and Breakfast in B.C., Box 24492, Station C, Vancouver, British Columbia V5T 4E1, Canada, (604) 946-7886, Helen Burich and Pauline Scoten.

Urban Ventures, 322 Central Park West, New York, NY 10025, (212) 662-1234, Frances Dworan and Mary McAulay.

Bridgeport. A mile from the Tennessee River and overlooking Crow Creek, this accommodation is in a secluded ranch-style home. The guest rooms have private entrances, and guests are invited to make use of the music room, which contains a grand piano and an organ. *Represented by:* Hospitality Plus Bed & Breakfast, AL-110, (205) 259-1298. $20–$30.

Crossville. A hospital dietitian, the host makes sure that guests are served a complete and nutritious breakfast. The guest rooms are on the third floor, which ensures privacy, and the host gladly assists guests in planning their activities. The area contains many flea markets and antique and woodworking shops. *Represented by:* Hospitality Plus Bed & Breakfast, AL-106, (205) 259-1298. $20–$30.

Decatur. Situated in the historic section of old Decatur, this late-nineteenth-century house is three blocks from the Tennessee River and convenient for shopping and restaurant dining. The hosts, a retired couple interested in genealogy and antiques, enjoy taking guests on walking tours to historic homes. *Represented by:* Hospitality Plus Bed & Breakfast, AL-103, (205) 259-1298. $20–$30.

Eva. Situated on 20 acres of Spivey Mountain, these two accommodations are both perfectly private: One house is a log cabin, with a mountain stream 10 feet from its front porch, and the other is modern, with a full kitchen. The hosts are retired business people interested in hiking and exploring, which perhaps explains their living only 15 miles from the Appalachian Trail. *Represented by:* Hospitality Plus Bed & Breakfast, (205) 259-1298. $20–$30.

Scottsboro. Your hosts, farmers interested in physical fitness, live in a farmhouse on the 1,200-acre Sand Mountain Farm. Interested in meeting farmers from other areas, they are also fond of showing guests the many impressive rock formations on their land. *Represented by:* Hospitality Plus Bed & Breakfast, AL-102, (205) 259-1298. $20–$25.

Section. Both of the guest rooms here have views of the Tennessee River winding through the Scottsboro area. The house is a ranch-style brick building on 10 acres of land. The hosts, retired teachers, serve guests a full Southern breakfast, complete with homemade jam and biscuits. *Represented by:* Hospitality Plus B & B, AL-105, (205) 259-1298. $24–$30.

Classical Musicians. A restored 1920s house hosted by classical musicians, this guest house offers an accommodation with exposed-beam ceilings, a Murphy bed, a private bath, a semiprivate entrance, and a breakfast room. *Represented by:* Bed & Breakfast Birmingham, (205) 591-6406. $24–$28.

Forest Park. Hosted by an ex-schoolteacher, this accommodation is on a tree-lined street in the historic Forest Park neighborhood. The guest room, which has twin beds, opens onto a small porch. *Represented by:* Bed & Breakfast Birmingham, (205) 591-6406. $24–$28.

Little Brick House. Conveniently located near Interstate 59, this guest house is hosted by a retired pharmaceutical-company representative and an accountant. The grounds are landscaped, and the guest room has twin beds. There is a fenced-in area outside for pets. *Represented by:* Bed & Breakfast Birmingham, (205) 591-6406. $28–$33.

Private Entrance. This furnished garage apartment features a private entrance, a kitchen, and a private bath with a claw-footed bathtub. The hosts are a retired teacher and a remodeling contractor. The lawn has a swing. *Represented by:* Bed & Breakfast Birmingham, (205) 591-6406. $28–$33.

Single Only. Conveniently located near Interstate 20, this modern home is hosted by a horticulturalist. The guest room has a private bath and jungle-pattern print wallpaper. The guest room has a private entrance, and enclosed parking is available. *Represented by:* Bed & Breakfast Birmingham, (205) 591-6406. $24.

Sauna. This guest house has a private entrance for guests, who are invited to use the pool and the sauna. The room has a kitchenette area. *Represented by:* Bed & Breakfast Birmingham, (205) 591-6406. $32–$40.

Ranch House. A rambling ranch house close to the center of town, this guest house has paneled basement quarters for guests. The accommodation has a double and a single bed, a separate entrance, a private bath, and a sitting room. The hosts, a retired banker and a librarian, welcome children if advance notice is given. *Represented by:* Bed & Breakfast Birmingham, (205) 591-6406. $28–$32.

The Brunton House

112 College Avenue, Scottsboro, AL 35768. (205) 259-1298. *Hosts:* Norman and Jerry Brunton.

The Brunton House, painted a light blue Williamsburg and trimmed in ivory and rust, was built in the mid-1920s. Jerry and Norman bought the house from the original owner's grandson and have maintained as many of its original appointments as possible.

The dining room has a bay window at one end and a fireplace. The living room, decorated with Tudor motifs in the tradition of English pubs, features rough texture walls and beams. Jerry and Norman got the idea for a bed-and-breakfast place after spending some time in England, which they feel they experienced more fully for having stayed with local families. They have also begun a bed-and-breakfast reservation service, for which they take reservations.

A second living room, there for the use of guests, has color television and a nonworking fireplace, whose artificial insert seems to give a pleasant glow to the room.

The first Monday of each month, and the Sunday before it, there is a First Monday Trade Day (one can find anything from soup to nuts and antiques as well) held two blocks from the Brunton House. This guest house is close to the Goosepond recreation area, which offers fishing, golf, swimming, and all manner of other outdoor activities.

Accommodations: 4 rooms with shared bath. *Smoking:* Permitted in living rooms only. *Children:* Permitted. *Pets:* Permitted outside if well behaved. *Driving Instructions:* Scottsboro is 41 miles from Huntsville on Route 72.

Gustavus Inn

Box 31, Gustavus, AK 99826. (907) 697-3311. *Hosts:* David and Joan Lesh.

Accessible only by airplane, the Gustavus Inn is a large structure that originally served as the homestead for a nine-child family. A generation later the building now functions as one of Alaska's few bed-and-breakfast places.

The Gustavus Inn is surrounded by Glacier Bay National Park, where you can observe icebergs, whales, seals sleeping on ice floes, mountain goats, and bald eagles. The park, which is the main attraction hereabouts, is awesomely beautiful.

The inn has a well-stocked bar and library, a working country kitchen, a wine and root cellar, and a greenhouse. The grounds run rife with wild berries, including strawberries, blueberries, and bog cranberries. The Salmon River, a hundred yards from the inn, yields plenty of cutthroat and Dolly Varden trout to fishermen.

The Leshes' rates include three meals, as well as airport-pick-up service. They serve fresh food, which in this part of the country means salmon, halibut, and crab. The vegetables are grown on their property and harvested daily.

Accommodations: 7 rooms with shared baths. *Smoking:* Permitted in lounge areas only. *Children:* Permitted. *Pets:* Permitted. *Breakfast:* Included. *Driving Instructions:* Accessible by plane only.

Skagway Inn

Seventh and Broadway, Box 483, Skagway, AK 99840. (907) 983-2289. *Hosts:* John and Janet O'Daniel.

Originally a saloon and dance hall, the Skagway Inn was built in 1897 and moved four blocks in 1916 to its present location. John and Janet bought the building in 1975 and then renovated it, naming the rooms after actual ladies of the evening, whose names they culled from police records. Two of these ladies owned pieces of the land the hotel currently sits on.

The lobby has its 1916 wainscoting still intact, and the lounge features a player piano, a banjo, a guitar, and a television set. The guest rooms feature such items as iron beds, mirrored dressers and bureaus, and a built-in buffet.

The O'Daniels don't serve meals, but their location is convenient to downtown Skagway, which is in the Klondike Gold Rush National Historical Park. Skagway (elevation 7,000 feet) has many nineteenth-century houses, curio shops, and gardens. The area's fishing and sight-seeing possibilities attract fishermen and naturalists from all over the world.

Accommodations: 15 rooms with shared baths. *Smoking:* Permitted. *Children:* Permitted. *Pets:* Permitted. *Driving Instructions:* In downtown Skagway.

Williams House Bed and Breakfast

420 Quapaw Avenue, Hot Springs National Park, AR 71901. (501) 624-4275. *Hosts:* Mary and Gary Riley.

Encircled by magnolia, oak, maple, and black walnut trees, with large holly bushes bordering one side of the property, this 1890 brownstone and brick Victorian house showed up in the National Register of Historic Places in 1978.

Inside the Williams House one discovers wainscoting, oak and walnut woodwork and doors, copper and brass antique lighting fixtures, beveled and stained-glass windows, cupid wall sconces, a 12-foot beveled mirror, a Franklin stove, a black marble fireplace, and other antique appointments too numerous to list. The house features such diversions as a piano, a game room with a color television set (cable), and several wraparound porches. All the guest rooms, furnished with antiques and plants, are centrally air-conditioned.

Mary and Gary serve a complimentary breakfast that's large enough for the biggest appetite—you can always have eggs with ham, bacon, or sausage and grits or hashed-brown potatoes; and when they're in the mood they rotate among eggs Benedict, French toast, omelets, waffles, pancakes, creamed eggs on toast, chipped beef, and other dishes.

Accommodations: 4 rooms, 2 with private bath. *Smoking:* Permitted in moderation. *Children:* Over 5 permitted. *Pets:* Not permitted. *Breakfast:* Included. *Driving Instructions:* From Little Rock, take Route I-30, then take Route 70 to Hot Springs.

Anchor Bay. One hundred miles north of San Francisco, this accommodation has a private deck that overlooks the ocean. The hosts' hobbies include photography and Chinese cooking. Represented by Northwest Bed & Breakfast, #500, (503) 246-8366 or 246-2383. $22–$30.

Aptos. The breakfast ingredients here come from the hosts' property, which is adjacent to a redwood forest and overlooks Monterey Bay. The house, in a rural area 10 miles south of Santa Cruz, is convenient to restaurants and tourist attractions and has a deck with a view. *Represented by:* Bed & Breakfast International, (415) 525-4569. $36.

Berkeley. A houseboat guest house? That's right. This accommodation, whose host is a professor interested in sailing, sits placidly in the Berkeley marina. There is bus service from the marina to the center of Berkeley, 3 miles away. *Represented by:* Northwest Bed & Breakfast, #503, (503) 246-8366 or 246-2383. $20.

Berkeley. The hostess, who speaks French, as well as English and some German and Italian, has a large repertoire of occupations—documentary filmmaker, editor, photographer. Her home, a Mediterranean-style villa on a hillside, features a fine view of San Francisco and the bay. One room has a private patio, and the grounds, contiguous with the Berkeley hills, contain a cactus-and-succulent garden, a fern collection, and many fruit trees. *Represented by:* Bed & Breakfast International, (415) 525-4569. $50.

Burbank. A retired teacher of music and art, the host of this accommodation frequently guides guests around the Hollywood studios, about which he knows a great deal. The house, on a quiet residential street, is a mile from the NBC studios. *Represented by:* Northwest Bed & Breakfast, #651, (503) 246-8366 or 246-2383. $22–$34.

Calistoga. The Larkmead offers four spacious guest rooms. The house is in a rural vineyard district, and a short walk will bring you to the Hans Kornell Champagne cellars or the Napa River. Breakfast is included; baths are shared. *Represented by:* Bed & Breakfast Exchange, (707) 963-7756. $60.

Chico. This contemporary home is beside a lake. The host is a fisherman, and the hostess plays banjo, piano, and guitar and sings with the "Sweet Adelines." Both are bridge players. They will pick up guests at the airport. *Represented by:* Northwest Bed & Breakfast, #509, (503) 246-8366 or 246-2383. $18–$32.

Healdsburg. Located in Healdsburg, one of the Sonoma Valley's smaller hamlets, the Grape Leaf is a Victorian guest house with four rooms, hosted by a young and vivacious lady who, in the afternoons, conducts casual wine tastings. The breakfast served to guests is a full one. *Represented by:* Bed & Breakfast Exchange, (707) 963-7756. $50–$60.

Hermosa Beach. The host, a high-school teacher interested in music and theater, has a home right on the Pacific shore. The ocean is just outside the front door, and the house's porch is perfect for watching sunsets. One guest room has a king-sized bed and a private bath with a Jacuzzi. *Represented by:* Bed & Breakfast International, (415) 525-4569. $36–$44.

Huntington Beach. This accommodation, 3 miles from the ocean and 30 minutes from Disneyland, features an outdoor pool, a covered patio, and parakeet aviaries. The hosts cultivate such hobbies as bridge, gardening, and golf. *Represented by:* Northwest Bed & Breakfast, #652, (503) 246-8366 or 246-2383. $18–$34.

La Jolla. The hostess, a high-school business teacher who works part time in real estate, offers guests a room, with a private bath, in her condominium, which has a pool and a Jacuzzi that guests may use. She enjoys sports and cooking, and her home is close to the University of California at San Diego and two new shopping centers. *Represented by:* Bed & Breakfast International, (415) 525-4569. $38.

Los Angeles. The host, a social worker, has two rooms for guests; but one of these is available only when her daughter is away at college. The house, on Comstock Avenue a short walk from Wilshire Boulevard, Beverly Hills, and UCLA, has a garden, which the main guest room overlooks. *Represented by:* Bed & Breakfast International, (415) 525-4569. $38.

Napa. A stunning Victorian guest house in downtown Napa, La Belle Epoque features elaborate stained-glass windows, a grand staircase, and a sun parlor. The hostess, a native of Chile, enhanced the decor of her home with many pieces of sculpture and oil paintings, as well as a collection of rare and unusual

La Belle Epoque, Napa (*Bed & Breakfast Exchange*)

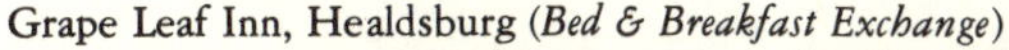

Grape Leaf Inn, Healdsburg (*Bed & Breakfast Exchange*)

Monterey, California (*Bed & Breakfast International*)

Monterey, California (*Bed & Breakfast International*)

plants and handmade antique furniture. *Represented by:* Bed & Breakfast Exchange, (707) 963-7756. $65–$85.

Napa Valley. Centrally located in the Napa Valley, La Residence is an 1850 three-story Victorian guest house with a spa on the premises. Seven guest rooms are available, and three of them have fireplaces. For those looking to get aloft, ballooning facilities are close by. *Represented by:* Bed & Breakfast Exchange, (707) 963-7756. $60–$90.

Newport Beach. Two hundred yards from a private swimming beach and an easy walk from the ferry to Catalina Island or Disneyland, this guest house is hosted by an attorney and his wife. The guest suite, which has a private entrance, includes two bedrooms and a sitting area with a fireplace and a refrigerator. *Represented by:* Bed & Breakfast International, (415) 525-4569. $44.

Palo Alto. This guest house, hosted by a counselor at Stanford University, was designed by the city architect of San Francisco. It has an inner courtyard with a patio surrounded by fig, persimmon, pear, and tangerine trees. The guest room has its own bath, and use of a hot tub can easily be arranged. *Represented by:* Bed & Breakfast International, (415) 525-4569. $36.

Pebble Beach. Surrounded by a pine and oak forest and adjacent to the Pebble Beach Golf Course, this house has a three-room suite available for guests. The suite contains a king-sized bed, television, a sitting room, a dining room with a kitchenette area, and a private bath. The house is convenient to restaurants and tourist attractions, and the hosts are interested in outdoor life and travel. *Represented by:* Bed & Breakfast International, (415) 525-4569. $44.

Pismo Beach. This guest house in a residential neighborhood across the street from a beach is hosted by an industrial-engineering teacher from California Polytechnic State University and a school nurse. Their home is 3 miles from shops and restaurants, and they enjoy offering dinner to their guests (for a moderate fee). *Represented by:* Bed & Breakfast International, (415) 525-4569. $36.

Pope Valley. Meadowcreek is a French country farmhouse with a walnut orchard in front and a vineyard in back. The entire house is available for guests. It features a swimming pool and two fireplaces—one in the master bedroom and the other in the living room. The master bedroom overlooks the vineyard. *Represented by:* Bed & Breakfast Exchange, (707) 963-7756. $100.

St. Helena. Situated just outside the city limits of St. Helena, Sandi's Place is a small cottage next to a Chardonnay vineyard. In season, vegetables from the property's garden may be sampled by guests. *Represented by:* Bed & Breakfast Exchange, (707) 963-7756. $30.

St. Helena. A Victorian guest house, the Cottage is within walking distance of St. Helena, which has several good restaurants and a host of interesting shops. The Cottage has kitchen facilities, a barbecue area, and two bicycles available for guests. *Represented by:* Bed & Breakfast Exchange, (707) 963-7756. $55.

St. Helena. Furnished with antiques, Morgan House is a contemporary guest cottage with a swimming pool and garden that guests are invited to use. The hostess serves breakfast to her guests. *Represented by:* Bed & Breakfast Exchange, (707) 963-7756. $65.

San Diego. This Tudor-style home in a residential neighborhood is close to many of San Diego's attractions, such as Mission Beach. The hosts, involved in library science and real estate, offer guests a room with a private entrance, a private bath, and television. *Represented by:* Bed & Breakfast International, (415) 525-4569. $40.

Sanger. Ten miles east of Fresno, this home features a view of the Sierra Nevadas and a swimming pool, which guests are invited to use. The host is a teacher. *Represented by:* Northwest Bed & Breakfast, #511, (503) 246-8366 or 246-2383. $20–$34.

Santa Cruz. The host, an attorney with a penchant for refinishing antique furniture and restoring vintage automobiles, has a ranch-style house that overlooks a golf course. *Represented by:* Northwest Bed & Breakfast, #512, (503) 246-8366 or 246-2383. $20–$30.

Sonoma. Located smack in the middle of the Sonoma wine country, the Campbell Ranch, a contemporary house, has facilities that include a pool and a tennis court. One of the hosts is involved in the wine industry, which perhaps explains why guests are offered fruit wine before retiring. (They're also offered homemade pie.) *Represented by:* Bed & Breakfast Exchange, (707) 963-7756. $50–$70.

Yountville. Situated in Yountville, a town that overlooks the Napa Valley, The Maddap House offers a tennis court, as well as spectacular views. Two guestrooms share a bath, and they also share a large living room with a bar and a fireplace. Another guest room features a private bath and a fireplace. The hosts are a doctor and his wife. *Represented by:* Bed & Breakfast Exchange, (707) 963-7756. $50–$70.

San Diego (*Bed & Breakfast International*)

The Rose Victorian Inn

789 Valley Road, Arroyo Grande, CA 93420. (408) 489-8398. *Hosts:* Diana and Ross Cox.

The Rose Victorian Inn is an 1885 Victorian–Italian stick structure (essentially Victorian but characterized by strong vertical and horizontal lines). Painted in five shades of red, the building takes up a full 1.5 acres, and the grounds include another 5 acres that haven't been, and won't be, developed. The patio area features a Jacuzzi and a sauna.

The living room has an inlaid onyx fireplace with a Chinese design, burgundy carpeting, a dragon-legged armchair hand-carved of ebony, a pump organ made of clear cedar stained dark, and a 13-foot ceiling with the house's original rosette and brass and a chandelier of hand-blown glass. The living room also has another fireplace, this one carved of oak, as well as a square rosewood grand piano that once belonged to General John C. Frémont. Off the living room there's a sun parlor done in white wicker with cushions upholstered in a burgundy fabric.

All the guest rooms are furnished with antiques. One room, which is 20 by 25 feet, has a mahogany armoire inlaid with oak and maple and is papered with silver, floral-print reproduction Victorian wallpaper. The bed is an antique, fashioned of brass and iron.

Hosts Diana and Ross met while in the third grade, but Diana tells me they didn't really become sweethearts until high school. Diana has a counseling and nursing background, and Ross used to be a contractor for Lion Country Safaris. (He built the largest natural-rock artificial waterfalls in the United States.)

Breakfast at the Rose Victorian is a treat: Such dishes as eggs Benedict and croissants stuffed with raisins and Parmesan cheese are parts of the typical morning meal.

Accommodations: 9 rooms, 5 with private bath. *Smoking:* Permitted outside only. *Children:* Under 16 not permitted. *Pets:* Not permitted. *Driving Instructions:* Take Route 101 north and exit at Arroyo Grande, then turn left at the stop sign (Fair Oaks), go ¼ mile, turn left on Valley Road, and proceed for another ¼ mile.

Berkeley **CALIFORNIA**

Gramma's Bed and Breakfast Inn

2740 Telegraph Avenue, Berkeley, CA 94705. (415) 549-2145. *Hostesses:* Suzanne and Dorothy Jackson.

This 1902 Tudor mansion with nine fireplaces, inlaid floors, leaded-glass windows, multilevel decks, and a formal English garden, is a large stone house smack in the middle of Berkeley.

Most rooms have fireplaces, private decks, and access to the garden. Eight have private entrances. All the guest rooms are furnished with antiques, and each bed is covered by a handmade quilt.

Gramma's owners boast that "there are no surprises when it comes to comfort and convenience." Evenings, the staff serves guests complimentary sherry or, in a longtime Gramma's tradition, cookies and milk. Suzanne and Dorothy Jackson also offer a Continental breakfast that includes freshly baked croissants, homemade preserves, and a pot of coffee.

If Gramma's accommodations don't succeed in spoiling you, its location will. Next door to the University of California at Bekeley, across the bridge from San Francisco, and almost adjacent to Tilden National Park, Gramma's tends, as Grammas do, to be close.

Accommodations: 19 rooms with private bath. *Smoking:* Permitted, but no cigars or pipes. *Children:* Over 6 permitted. *Pets:* Not permitted. *Breakfast:* Included. *Driving Instructions:* Take Route I-80 to Ashby turnoff, which runs into Telegraph Avenue; go three blocks.

Carmel **CALIFORNIA**

Holiday House

Camino Real at Seventh, Carmel, California. *Mailing Address:* P.O. Box 234, Carmel, CA 93921. (408) 624-6267. *Hosts:* Kenneth and Janet Weston.

A five-minute walk from the beach, Holiday House is a 1905 brown shingled cottage with dormered windows on its upper floor, sun parlor, and a terrace that overlooks the garden. The house was originally built as a summer cottage by a professor from Stanford University, and in the 1920s two sisters from Kansas bought the place and began the guest-house operation that has been going on under various owners ever since.

The living room features a large stone fireplace, views of the ocean and the garden, a plethora of books and games, and a grand piano. The furnishings include antique pieces, as well as many original works by local artists.

Three of the guest rooms have ocean views, and the other three overlook the garden. The upstairs rooms have slanted ceilings, and Kenneth and Janet make sure that all the guest rooms have ample supplies of fresh flowers and jelly beans.

Kenneth and Janet serve guests complimentary sherry and offer a breakfast that comes with homemade coffee cake or muffins. Their location is convenient to everything in Carmel: The town, with its galleries, shops, and restaurants, and the beach.

Accommodations: 6 rooms, 2 with private bath. *Smoking:* Permitted on the terrace. *Children:* Under 6 not permitted. *Pets:* Not permitted. *Breakfast:* Included. *Driving Instructions:* Take the Ocean Avenue exit off Route 1, continue on Ocean through town to Camino Real, turn left, and Holiday house will be on the right, just before Seventh Avenue.

Carmel **CALIFORNIA**

San Antonio House

P.O. Box 3683, Carmel, CA 93921. (408) 624-4334. *Hosts:* Michael and Joan Cloran.

San Antonio House is a large, shingled turn-of-the-century house with flowered patios and a sizable lawn. An old Monterey Pine, at least 4 feet in diameter, almost touches one corner of the house.

Of the house's two owners, Michael Cloran used to be a stockbroker and his wife, Joan, an interior designer and art collector. Michael feels that totally changing their life-styles is the best move he and his wife ever made. Lola Fuess helps them as manager.

San Antonio House offers three guest suites, all of them with a private entrance, television set, and a refrigerator. One suite, on the top floor, has three rooms and a view of the ocean. The guest-room furnishings include antiques, bright fabrics, and paintings and photographs from Michael and Joan's collection. There are paintings by Van Gogh and Lautrec, photographs of Europe, and books everywhere.

Michael and Joan don't serve guests breakfast, but the refrigerator in each suite is stocked with fresh orange juice and coffee. Finding sustenance is easy in Carmel, which is only three blocks from San Antonio House.

Accommodations: 3 suites with private bath. *Smoking:* Permitted. *Children:* Permitted. *Pets:* Permitted. *Breakfast:* Fruit juice and coffee included. *Driving Instructions:* Take Route 1 to Ocean Avenue in Carmel near the beach; the house is on San Antonio Avenue between Ocean and Seventh.

Vintage Towers

302 North Main Street, Cloverdale, CA 95425. (707) 894-4535. *Hosts:* Tom and Judy Hayworth.

A Victorian, Queen Anne tower house with three turrets (one round, one square, and one octagonal), Vintage Towers is at the corner of two wide and quiet residential streets. A wisteria-covered veranda looks out on a garden that yields roses the size of grapefruits and whose pomegranate, persimmon, plum, apple, cherry, and other trees enclose the grounds almost completely. The garden also has a gazebo, which Tom built.

The ground-floor parlor has a golden oak piano, an antique mahogany Pianola, a solid-oak griffin rocking chair and a maroon Oriental rug with a pattern in light blue and black. The entire ground floor is wainscoted in clear fir, and the library, with more than a thousand volumes, is always open to guests. The dining room, a rather formal one, has leaded-glass windows overlooking the garden and reflecting the fireplace on the wall opposite.

Each guest room has a theme. One actually has a carousel horse in it, another is done in dark reds and furnished with dark woods, and another has a private terrace and a sitting area. All the rooms are furnished with antiques.

Accommodations: 6 rooms, 2 with private bath. *Smoking:* Permitted on the veranda and the balcony only. *Children:* Under 10 not permitted. *Pets:* Not permitted. *Breakfast:* Included. *Driving Instructions:* Vintage Towers is one block east of Route 101 in the town of Cloverdale, at the corner of Third and Main streets.

Bud and Dot Shackelford

11532 Rolling Hills Drive, El Cajon, CA 92020. (714) 442-3164. *Hosts:* Bud and Dot Shackelford.

This is the house that Bud built, and designed and architected. Dot considers it her husband's best work of art, although the Grumbacher and Strathmore companies, who sponsor Bud's annual demonstration and workshop tours throughout the United States, might disagree.

The grounds seem almost overrun by trees—eighteen avocados, six oranges, a lemon, a lime, a grapefruit, a tangelo, and a pecan, most of which produce year-round. A large wooden deck with a view in three directions runs around the house. The living room and family room walls have rough cedar paneling, and the exposed cedar-beam ceilings in the center of the house go as high as 15 feet. The house, most of it carpeted wall-to-wall, features large glass windows and sliding doors, a fireplace with Italian black marble trim, and an unobstructed view of 50 miles.

The Shackelfords include a complimentary full breakfast including tree-fresh orange juice and homemade marmalade. Guests may swim in their pool.

Accommodations: 4 rooms, 1 with private bath. *Smoking:* Permitted. *Children:* Permitted. *Pets:* Not permitted. *Breakfast:* Included. *Driving Instructions:* Rolling Hills Drive is 10 minutes from El Cajon and 30 minutes from San Diego.

Ferndale **CALIFORNIA**

The Priory Guesthouse

705 Washington Street, Ferndale, CA 95536. (707) 786-9157; 786-9158. *Hosts:* Captain Edward J. Ward and David Farrow.

Sparing no expense, Bishop Hurley in 1963 ordered The Priory built as a convent. The contemporary brick building, now a guest house, is surrounded by rolling lawns, fruit trees, and flower gardens. Horses graze in the bottom pasture, and sheep roam an adjoining field.

What used to be the confessional is now a well-stocked bar that, though not yet licensed to sell liquor, offers complimentary wine and after-dinner drinks. Every once in a while, guests get to savor homemade blackberry liquor. What used to be the convent's chapel serves as a sitting room, heated on cool nights by a large stone fireplace. What used to be the nuns' sitting room is a library with plenty of books, a generous selection of English magazines, a fireplace, and here and there, bowls of wildflowers.

Captain Ward and David Farrow bring English tea or coffee and fresh orange juice to their guests each morning, and after these and their morning paper, guests usually partake of the full country breakfast served in the Priory Restaurant, a short stroll down the road.

Accommodations: 6 rooms with shared baths. *Smoking:* Permitted but not in bedrooms. *Children:* Not permitted. *Pets:* Not permitted. *Breakfast:* Included. *Driving Instructions:* From San Francisco, take Route 101 North to the Ferndale-Fernbridge exit, go 5 miles into Ferndale, and turn left on Washington Street.

Isis Oasis Lodge and Cultural Center

20889 Geyserville Avenue, Geyserville, CA 95441. (707) 857-3524. *Hosts:* Lorna Vigne and Paul Ramses.

When the San Francisco city legislature passed a law forbidding its residents to harbor exotic animals, Lorna Vigne—who happened to own six ocelots, three bush babies, and a tarantula—decided to move. She has led a life that seems to strain coincidence: her achievements in San Francisco include presiding over the birth of the first ocelot ever born in that city, as well as running, out of a work-home complex of buildings, the Nori Enamelcraft Company.

The Isis Oasis comprises several buildings on a large parcel of land. The grounds include a mini-zoo, a pool, a sauna, and a meditation tree—a four-hundred-year-old Douglas fir whose trunk has divided three times. The parlor, with a fireplace in the middle and a view of the pool, features a billiard table and other diversions.

The guest rooms are furnished, as Lorna says, in country exotic. There's plenty of bamboo, plants, wood, white walls, and Indian bedspreads.

In addition to running a guest house that offers complimentary wine and breakfast, Lorna has founded a group called the Isis Society for Inspirational Studies. She and the society's director—Paul Ramses, a Past Life Therapist—conduct workshops.

Lorna calls her facilities "not a motel, but rather a sharing of a very special place on our planet."

Accommodations: 12 rooms with shared baths. *Smoking:* Permitted. *Children:* Permitted. *Pets:* Tolerated. *Breakfast:* Included. *Driving Instructions:* From San Francisco, take Route 101 to the Geyserville exit; the lodge's driveway is the second on the left.

The Heirloom

214 Shakeley Lane, Ione, CA 95640. (205) 274-4468. *Hostesses:* Patricia Cross and Melisande Hubbs.

The Heirloom is an 1863 two-story brick Colonial structure, situated on 1.5 acres of private grounds. Magnolia, crepe myrtle, chinaberry and walnut trees totally enclose the lawn, which has four sets of chairs and umbrellaed tables and a small white gazebo.

The ground-floor parlor—where complimentary sherry, tea, or coffee is always available for guests—contains a rosewood piano that once belonged to Lola Montez, a 400-year-old refectory table from Italy, an elaborately hand-carved chest made entirely of teak in China, and a wood-burning fireplace surrounded by overstuffed sofas and wing chairs upholstered in a brilliant Williamsburg blue.

One guest room has a private bath, a working fireplace with a reproduction of an early Degas hanging from the brick wall above it, a walnut Eastlake bed with a matching dresser and two French doors that open onto a semiprivate balcony, which overlooks the lawn. Another room has a brass bed and a private balcony, with chairs, a love seat, and a table, that faces the tops of 75-year-old trees.

Pat (a former housewife, missionary, and business manager) and Sandy (previously a registered nurse and a housewife) serve a generous complimentary breakfast. The fare includes cheese and sour-cream crepes, hot popovers, freshly squeezed orange juice, fresh fruit, and home-ground coffee. Pat and Sandy, in period costumes, serve their guests breakfast in bed.

Accommodations: 4 rooms, 1 with private bath. *Smoking:* Permitted. *Children:* Permitted. *Pets:* Not permitted. *Breakfast:* Included. The Heirloom is in the center of Ione.

Ann Marie's Lodgin and Gallery

410 Stasal Street, Jackson, CA 95642. (209) 223-1452. *Hostess:* Ann Marie Joseph.

Ann Marie, a pretty and seemingly indefatigable hostess, says, "Actually I'm very tame; just don't track in any mud, let your young 'uns break my chamberpot, or throw up on my critter [her little son Herbert], and I'll most likely let ya have your way."

Ann Marie, an artist who works in acrylics, charcoal, pencil, and pen and ink, also writes articles for *Off Road* magazine. She sometimes sketches on the baseboards of her house. The kitchen features a cartoon sketch of Herbert, his head and a bunch of bubbles rising from a bathtub. Ann Marie also grows most of her own food and puts up her own preserves. The "grub . . . 9 A.M." is a complimentary breakfast that includes fruits in season, juice, meat pie, and brandy.

The 1892 Victorian house is furnished mostly with pieces from her grandparents' farm. Her paintin's and sketchin's cover the holes in the walls, she observes.

Ann Marie got the idea for a bed-and-breakfast place because she "was often refused lodgin' while travelin' with my children, because they were little folks. And also 'cause I like to eat, and ya know, my critters got the same likes." Unlike the many hosts who don't allow children, Ann Marie will critter-sit for her guests.

Accommodations: 3 rooms with private bath. *Smoking:* Permitted in the parlor only. *Children:* Permitted. *Pets:* Permitted outside only. *Breakfast:* Included. *Driving Instructions:* Take Route 49 to North Main Street; turn right at the first stoplight, and right at the first intersection, which is Stasal Street.

Jackson **CALIFORNIA**

The Court Street Inn

215 Court Street, Jackson, CA 95642. (209) 223-0416. *Hostess:* Mildred Burns.

The California State Historic Resources Commission recently designated the Court Street Inn a "State Point of Historic Interest" and recommended that the building be placed in the National Register of Historic Places. The facade is typical of nineteenth-century gold-country architecture; but once you step inside you won't encounter anything merely typical.

The parlor, where guests are served complimentary sherry, has a white marble fireplace, a black ebony Chinese screen with a bird pattern inlaid in stones of various shades (jades and soapstones primarily), a hand-carved Belter couch upholstered in a pink brocade fabric, a beige-and-pink Oriental rug, a marble-topped Eastlake table, and a Hong Kong chest made of camphor wood with hundreds of tiny figurines carved at least half an inch in relief.

One ground-floor guest room contains Eastlake spoon-carved furniture, a beige Oriental rug with a tree-of-life pattern in shades of rust, a wood-burning fireplace, a marble-topped dresser with a mirror, an antique desk, and a collection of antique photographs. Another ground-floor guest room is furnished with Queene Ann pieces, and has a magenta Oriental rug and a floral-design rose-colored wallpaper. The room also has a sun-parlor sitting area with three exposures, furnished with rattan and carpeted in a brilliant green. Of the five guest rooms, three have private baths, and the other two, each with its own half bath, share a water closet that contains a large claw-footed tub fitted with a brass shower apparatus.

The complimentary breakfast here is as varied and sumptuous as the furnishings.

Accommodations: 5 rooms, 3 with private bath. *Smoking:* Permitted. *Children:* Not permitted. *Pets:* Not permitted. *Breakfast:* Included. *Driving Instructions:* From Jackson take Main Street to Court Street and drive up the hill.

Laguna Beach **CALIFORNIA**

Carriage House

1322 Catalina Street, Laguna Beach, CA 92651. (714) 494-8945. *Hosts:* Vernon and Dee Taylor.

A designated historical landmark, the Carriage House is a 1920 Colonial-style structure. The cupola on the roof was added by Louis B. Mayer (the second *M* in MGM) when he owned the building, which is a five-minute walk from the Pacific Ocean.

The Carriage House features a central courtyard with a brick floor and a profusion of plants and flowers—some on hanging planters, some in ornate ground-level pots, some in huge built-in brick planters. Moss hangs from a gnarled carrotwood tree.

Each guest suite has a sitting room and a separate bedroom—some have two bedrooms, some have fully equipped kitchens. Decor combines antiques and modern furnishings, and plants seem to be everywhere.

Guests find a complimentary bottle of California wine and a bowl of fresh fruit waiting for them in their suites. Afternoon refreshment is always available in Grandma Fean's Dining Room, whose carved-wood chairs and antique chests seem the perfect backdrop for the family-style complimentary breakfast.

Accommodations: 6 suites with private bath. *Smoking:* Permitted. *Children:* Permitted. *Pets:* Permitted if well behaved. *Breakfast:* Included. *Driving Instructions:* From Laguna take the Coast Highway south to Cress Street, turn east to Catalina Street.

Little River **CALIFORNIA**

Glendeven

8221 North Highway 1, Little River, CA 95456. (707) 937-0083. *Hosts:* Jan and Janet De Vries.

Two miles south of Mendocino and adjacent to Van Damme State Park, Glendeven is an 1867 New England–style house. Eucalyptus trees shade the garden, where such flowers as camellias, princess flowers, and a rare acacia bloom in their proper seasons. A path winds through the state park to the ocean, its shore ruggedly beautiful in this part of the country.

Jan and Janet De Vries both have backgrounds in art and contemporary crafts, and their house shows it. Tasteful posters—a Georgia O'Keeffe here, the Cloisters's unicorn series there—as well as strong contemporary paintings and ceramics, catch the eye continually. The artwork blends effortlessly with the many green plants.

The sitting room, where Janet serves a complimentary breakfast of freshly baked muffins, fresh fruit, juice, coffee, and eggs, has a dark mahogany baby-grand piano, a sofa-and-chair set covered in Belgian linen, a fireplace, and some 20-odd feet of windows facing south. Oriental rugs lie on a subtle puce-gray carpet. One guest room has a fireplace and French doors that open onto a private balcony; another has a slanted wall with two skylights.

Accommodations: 6 rooms, 4 with private bath. *Smoking:* Permitted in the sitting room only. *Children:* Permitted only by prior arrangement. *Pets:* Not permitted. *Breakfast:* Included. *Driving Instructions:* On Route 1, located 2 miles south from Mendocino.

Little River **CALIFORNIA**

Victorian Farmhouse

P.O. Box 357, 7001 Highway 1, Little River, CA 95456. (707) 937-0697. *Hosts:* Tom and Jane Szilasi.

The Victorian Farmhouse was built in 1877 by John and Emma Dora Dennen, who came to this area from Maine, as many pioneers did. The grounds, which occupy several acres, include an apple orchard and flower gardens.

The inn is several hundred yards from the ocean, and some of the rooms, two of which feature redwood ceilings, have ocean views. Another room overlooks a private flower garden, and one suite features a French wood-burning stove and a sitting room. All rooms, as well as the public areas, are furnished with antiques.

The main parlor has a fireplace and, not far away, a decanter of sherry to keep guests warm. Victorian living room upstairs overlooks the flower garden.

The Szilasis bring a complimentary breakfast of juice, coffee or tea, fresh fruit, and hot breads and muffins to their guests' rooms each morning.

Accommodations: 4 rooms with private bath. *Smoking:* Permitted. *Children:* Over 16 permitted. *Pets:* Not permitted. *Breakfast:* Included. *Driving Instructions:* On Route 1, 2½ miles south of Mendocino.

Casa Lorrande

2200 Pacific Coast Highway, Malibu, CA 90265. (213) 456-9333. *Hosts:* Jim and Charlou Lorrande.

A thirty-year-old, 4,000-square-foot house, Casa Lorrande has had many tenants, including Lee Marvin, Ben Gazzara, Laurence Harvey, Jayne Mansfield, Connie Stevens, Judy Garland, John Travolta, and Rodney Dangerfield. Perhaps these movie stars moved into the house because of the neighbors: Johnny Carson, Flip Wilson, Jennifer Jones, and Carol Burnett have homes in the same strip of beach. Locals call the area Millionaire's Row.

If show business bores you, you can look at the stars overhead or watch the sun sink into the Pacific. Even those who loathe California's tinsel and glamour have to admit the place looks gorgeous when you have your back to it and are squinting at an ocean horizon bisecting a blood-orange sun.

John and Charlou have plants growing two stories high in the stairwell. The living room has a fireplace, a library, and exposed beams in the ceiling. The master bedroom also has a fireplace, as well as 40 feet of windows facing the ocean. The property features a 60-foot private beach overlooked by an ocean porch where you may have your complimentary breakfast if you like.

Accommodations: 3 rooms with private bath. *Smoking:* Permitted. *Children:* Permitted. *Pets:* Permitted occasionally, check first. *Breakfast:* Included. *Driving Instructions:* Drive 12 miles north from Santa Monica on the Pacific Coast Highway.

Mendocino **CALIFORNIA**

The Headlands Inn

44950 Albion Street, Mendocino, CA 95460. (707) 937-4431. *Hosts:* Pete Albrecht, Lynn Anderson, and Kathy Casper.

A few hundred yards from the Pacific Ocean, on a hill that overlooks it, is The Headlands Inn, a restored 1868 Victorian building painted ivory and trimmed in brown. It was originally a barber shop but was reincarnated over the years as a saloon, a hotel annex, a private residence, and, currently, a bed-and-breakfast inn.

The three front guest rooms—all have fireplaces, and one has bay windows—face directly on the ocean and the Mendocino coastline with its blue water and white surf and rugged mountains. The third-floor guest rooms feature redwood window seats in dormer windows, and a second-floor room has a parlor stove on a round hearth backed by glistening copper. Another room opens onto a private balcony that overlooks the ocean as well as the town of Mendocino.

Beige carpeting runs throughout the halls and the guest rooms, framed antique maps hang everywhere, and tiny Victorian print wallpapers and dark woods are prominent in the decor. Every quilt in the place was made by hand; fresh flowers are on every breakfast tray and in every room.

Pete, Lynn, and Kathy bring a complimentary breakfast to your room; if you like, they will start a fire for you if your room has a fireplace. "It's a lot of work," says Lynn, "but the people are worth it."

Accommodations: 5 rooms with private bath. *Smoking:* Permitted. *Children:* Over 16 permitted. *Pets:* Not permitted. *Breakfast:* Included. *Driving Instructions:* From Cloverdale, take Route 128 to Route 1 North; exit at Mendocino and proceed to Albion Street.

Monterey **CALIFORNIA**

The Jabberwock

598 Laine Street, Monterey, CA 93940. (408) 375-4777. *Hosts:* Jim and Barbara Allen.

Named after Lewis Carroll's famous poem, the Jabberwock is a 1911 neo-Victorian gabled structure painted cream and forest green. The house, which was a Roman Catholic convent during its first thirty years, has several porches, one of which wraps around its bay side and overlooks the water. The grounds contain two 20- by 50-foot waterfalls, one of which has five streams feeding three tiered pools.

The living room has a brick fireplace, forest-green wall-to-wall carpeting, furnishings from the 1920s, and wainscoting painted cream. The dining room, which faces Montery Bay, also has a fireplace, as well as an oaken floor on which is an Oriental rug in shades of maroon.

The 15- by 35-foot Borogrove Room ("All mimsy were the borogroves") features a mahogany king-sized bed with four down pillows, a down comforter, and percale sheets with lace borders; a fireplace; dark forest-green wall-to-wall carpeting; and a Victorian love seat and chair upholstered in a delicate tapestry fabric. The third-floor guest rooms, which overlook the bay, have slanted ceilings covered with reproduction Victorian print wallpapers.

Host Jim Allen, who has been involved in at least thirty restorations, is a fireman; and Barbara has been active in the hotel business for 15 years. Jim and Barbara supply guests with bathrobes, complimentary wine and hors d'oeuvres, fresh flowers, and other amenities such as shoe-polishing service.

Accommodations: 4 rooms, 1 with private bath. *Smoking:* Permitted. *Children:* Not permitted. *Pets:* Not permitted. *Breakfast:* Included. *Driving Instructions:* Take Route 68 west to Route 1 South, exit at Monterey, and then turn right at Camino Aguajito, left at Del Monte, and left again at Hoffman.

The Beazley House

1910 First Street, Napa, CA 94558. (707) 257-1649. *Hosts:* Jim and Carol Beazley.

Nicely shaded by the large, mature maple trees distributed about its front lawn, the Beazley House is a 1902 Colonial Revival house with a hipped roof. A large oak tree shades the entire backyard, where guests often relax.

The ground-floor parlor, where guests are always welcome, has a fireplace, two Prussian blue wing chairs, an overstuffed couch covered in beige linen with a blue-and-green floral pattern, and a brass serving cart stocked with complimentary sherry and a variety of teas. Adjoining the parlor is a library and music room. Guests are invited to use the stereo (except in the morning, when it plays Mozart during breakfast) or to read any of the more than four hundred volumes in the library, which, Jim being a former photo journalist, contains an extensive collection of photography books.

The foyer is dominated by the blue Persian rug on its hardwood floor and the large oaken staircase leading to the second floor. The stairs are carpeted in a dark powder blue, and six steps or so above the foyer, on the staircase's landing, there's a stained-glass inset of rich orange roses on a Tiffany blue background 6 feet in diameter.

Accommodations: 6 rooms with shared baths. *Smoking:* Not permitted. *Children:* Under 12 not permitted. *Pets:* Not permitted. *Breakfast:* Included. *Driving Instructions:* The house is in central Napa, at the corner of First and Warren streets.

Yesterhouse Inn

643 Third Street, Napa, CA 94559. (707) 257-0550. *Hosts:* Susan and Jack Harrison and Paula Weir.

Yesterhouse Inn is an 1896 Queen Anne Victorian house with small orange trees in its yard and a rose garden between its main building and two guest cottages.

One host used to be an electronics draftsman with Hewlett Packard, and another runs a group interested in antiques that meets each week at the inn.

The front parlor has a chandelier, a white marble fireplace, a red Victorian loveseat, red-floral-on-white Victorian wallpaper, red-on-red drapes over white linen curtains, and a red, ivory, and turquoise Oriental rug. The library (as is the rest of the house, furnished with antiques) contains more than six hundred books on antiques. The sun porch has a brown and tan Persian rug on the floor, many hanging plants, and a lace-covered table surrounded by four bentwood chairs. Hand-carved beds appear in most guest rooms, and every quilt and afghan in the house is handmade.

The rates here include a complimentary breakfast of pastries and breads, fresh fruit, and coffee or tea. Complimentary wine is served each evening.

Accommodations: 6 rooms, 3 with private bath. *Smoking:* Permitted. *Children:* Tolerated. *Pets:* Not permitted. *Breakfast:* Included. *Driving Instructions:* From Silverado Trail, take Third Street west to its intersection with Burnell.

Valley View Citrus Ranch

14801 Avenue 428, Orosi, CA 93647. (209) 528-2275. *Hosts:* Tom and Ruth Flippen.

Surrounded by three olive trees, twenty-six bougainvillea vines, and a hundred or so geranium plants, the Valley View Citrus Ranch is a 1964 structure, with Spanish or Mexican design overtones. Several of the bathrooms and the kitchen have Spanish tiles. Encircled by orange, peach, and avocado orchards, the grounds contain two patios and a 70-foot porch. The Valley View is a working orchard ranch that produces, primarily, oranges and ruby-red seedless grapes.

The living room, which has a brick fireplace, overstuffed furniture upholstered in shades of green, and wood-paneled walls, overlooks a valley, and on a clear day you can see the ocean. One guest room features Indian wall hangings, a private entrance, a private bath, a king-size bed, and wall-to-wall carpeting.

On the grounds are a clay tennis court and a trailer, which Ruth told me she and Tom stayed in during a period when they had an overflow of guests.

Ruth serves either a Continental or a full breakfast, depending on her guests' preferences.

Accommodations: 4 rooms, 2 with private bath. *Smoking:* Permitted. *Children:* Permitted. *Pets:* Permitted if arranged for *far* in advance. *Breakfast:* Included. *Driving Instructions:* The house is 8 miles east of Denuba on El Monte (Avenue 416). Follow El Monte to Route 144, then go north 2 miles to Avenue 428, turn right, and go ¾ mile to the house on the hill.

The Gosby House Inn

643 Lighthouse Avenue, Pacific Grove, CA 93953. (408) 375-1390. *Hosts:* Roger and Sally Post.

In search of a climate warmer than that of his native Nova Scotia, P. F. Gosby traveled to California and decided to settle in Pacific Grove, a small city on the Monterey Peninsula. Gosby built this Victorian mansion in 1887, and operated it as a boardinghouse for Methodist church members who attended summer retreats in Pacific Grove. When the only other hotel in the area burned down, Gosby began to expand his house.

The house, now in the National Register of Historic Places, has been totally restored—its original stained glass and wood moldings seem almost new. Guest rooms, several of which have fireplaces, are all furnished with antiques and have quilts, silk flowers, ruffled curtains, and reproduction wallpapers.

A Continental breakfast is served each morning in the parlor, or guests may want to take their breakfasts to the backyard, the front porch, or their rooms. Each afternoon, complimentary sherry, apple cider, and tea are served.

Accommodations: 19 rooms, 13 with private bath. *Smoking:* Not permitted. *Children:* Over 12 tolerated. *Pets:* Not permitted. *Driving Instructions:* Take Route 1 to the Pebble Beach–17 Mile Drive turnoff; turn right onto Route 68 and follow it to Forest Avenue in Pacific Grove; continue on Forest to Lighthouse Avenue, then turn left and go three blocks.

Green Gables Inn

104 Fifth Street, Pacific Grove, CA 93950. (408) 375-2095.
Hosts: Sally and Roger Post.

This 1888 Victorian building is, as its name suggests, a many-gabled structure with leaded-glass windows here and there and an intricate brickwork chimney and chapel. The house overlooks Monterey Bay, one of the Pacific Ocean's more pacific inlets. A small cove beach is directly across the road from the inn.

The guest rooms, decorated with antiques and reproduction wallpapers, contain such niceties as window seats. One room has a ladder leading to a small attic that faces the ocean. The downstairs rooms—a large living room for guests, a den, a dining room, and a kitchen—feature high ceilings, stained-glass windows, and breathtaking views.

Sally and Roger Post serve a complimentary breakfast each morning, happily make dinner reservations for guests, and always make sure to direct them to areas of special interest.

Accommodations: 5 rooms with shared baths; open June 15 through August 1. *Smoking:* Not permitted. *Children:* Over 12 tolerated. *Pets:* Not permitted. *Driving Instructions:* Take Route 1 to the Pebble Beach—17 Mile Drive exit; turn right onto Route 58; continue to Forest Avenue in Pacific Grove; follow it to Ocean View Boulevard and turn right; continue to Fifth Street.

Placerville **CALIFORNIA**

The Fleming Jones Homestead

3170 Newton Road, Placerville, CA 95667. *Hostess:* Janice Condit.

In 1883, Fleming Jones, a homesteader who seldom gambled, won a great deal of money. Slapping the cash down on the table, the story goes, he said to his wife, "There, go build your new house." Fleming and Florence Jones transformed their gambling windfall into a farmhouse built entirely of clear lumber and surrounded it with a large lawn bordered by a wall of hand-hewn stones. The homestead comprises 11 acres of meadows and woods.

From the outside the Fleming Jones Homestead appears to be a working farm, and it is. Chickens and hens roam the property, either ignoring guests or looking for a handout; four antique burros, willing to be ridden after they've dined, graze in the meadows. To keep it from awakening the guests at 4:30 A.M., the owner locks the rooster in the barn.

From the inside the homestead appears to be a rare cache of antiques and artwork. The dining room has a 54- by 138-inch oaken table supported by carved griffin legs. The central parlor, where guests gravitate toward complimentary sherry or tea, has two Morris rockers upholstered in a fabric of dusty rose, a curved Chinese bed-table made entirely of teak, and several paintings by Olga de Chica, the celebrated Colombian primitive.

One guest room combines a 6-foot carved-oak headboard, walls covered with pale yellow wainscoting, and a series of etchings the owner picked up while teaching English in South America.

Another guest room has walls covered almost entirely by framed pressed-flower collages assembled by the owner's great-uncle, a botanist. The walls in the Lovers Fancy room are peach and match the peach and ivory fabric of the room's two corner screens as well as the comforter that covers an iron and brass bed.

Janice Condit tries to make her place "A retreat, where city people can escape the craziness, wander in the woods, get back in touch with themselves, you know."

Accommodations: 3 rooms, 1 with private bath. *Smoking:* Permitted. *Children:* Not permitted. *Pets:* Not permitted. *Breakfast:* Included. *Driving Instructions:* Take Route 50 to Newton Road and turn right just past the pond.

Britt House

406 Maple Street, San Diego, CA 92103. (714) 234-2926.

Hosts: Daun Martin, Charlene Brown, and Robert Hostick. Britt House, a white 1887 Victorian building, was built by an attorney and has served over the years as everything from a teahouse to a chiropractor's office. The grounds contain a formal garden, from which come the flowers that decorate every room.

The entrance hall has an ornate staircase, and behind it there's a stained-glass window the size of a wall—a triptych that depicts morning, afternoon, and evening primarily with blue, red, green, and opal glass. The window catches the afternoon sun and lights the entrance way like a Chinese lantern. The parlor has a nonworking tiled fireplace, a carved Victorian couch upholstered in a rust velour, and light and dark rust reproduction Victorian print wallpaper.

The guest rooms have reproduction Victorian wallpapers, hardwood floors, and antique furnishings. One guest room has a sofa that used to belong to Ludwig, the "mad" king of Bavaria. There's also a small cottage, which has a kitchenette, a private bath, and quite a few antique pieces, primarily made of oak. One of the bathrooms has a sauna, which guests are invited to use.

Guests are greeted with a complimentary glass of wine, and each room contains fresh fruit and candies. Breakfast (juice, breads, a soft-boiled egg, and coffee) is brought to your room.

Accommodations: 8 rooms with shared baths. *Smoking:* Permitted. *Children:* Check in advance. *Pets:* Not permitted. *Breakfast:* Included. *Driving Instructions:* From I-5 take the airport exit onto Kettner Boulevard, go 1 mile, turn left on Laurel and again on third, and turn right on Fourth, which runs into Maple.

San Francisco
Victorian
(Bed & Breakfast International)

Guerrero Street. The Mission Dolores section of San Francisco contains a number of Victorian structures that escaped the great earthquake and fire of 1906. This one, which used to be the Spanish Consulate, is an Italianate building on a knoll, set well back from the street. One of the hosts is an elementary-school teacher with an interest in interior design, and the other markets computers. *Represented by:* Bed & Breakfast International, (415) 525-4569. $44.

Sixth Avenue. A short walk from Golden Gate State Park, this turn-of-the-century three-story house features a 12- by 24-foot combined bedroom and sitting room with antique furnishings, a private bath, and television. Another room features a stereo, television, and a sitting area. Street parking is available. *Represented by:* Bed & Breakfast International, (415) 525-4569. $36–$44.

Fillmore Street. Half a block from Union Street (one of San Francisco's more fashionable thoroughfares), this guest house offers two rooms, one of which has a sun deck and a view of the Golden Gate Bridge. The hosts, one in real estate and the other a homemaker, have two teenage children, a boy and a girl, living at home. *Represented by:* Bed & Breakfast International, (415)525-4569. $36–$44.

Greenwich Street. A business consultant and a computer information manager, the hosts have a 1920s home at the top of Russian Hill, down which cable cars roll to the bay. The guest room has an Oriental rug and a private bath, and the hosts bring breakfast to their guests' bedroom. *Represented by:* Bed & Breakfast International, (415) 525-4569. $44.

Sutter Street. Built in 1889 by Colonel Isaac Trumbo, this house is one of San Francisco's historic homes. The guest suite has a private bath, a dining room with television, and a kitchen. The hosts are a school principal and an educational-agency worker, and their home is within walking distance of downtown San Francisco. *Represented by:* Bed & Breakfast International, (415) 525-4569. $40.

San Francisco Victorian
(*Bed & Breakfast International*)

The Bed and Breakfast Inn

4 Charlton Court, San Francisco, CA 94123. (415) 921-9784. *Hosts:* Marily and Bob Kavanaugh.

On a quiet, mews-type street in the middle of one of San Francisco's most fashionable areas, The Bed and Breakfast Inn is a beautifully restored pair of adjacent Victorian town houses.

One suite has a private balcony, a living room, a kitchen, and a carpeted spiral staircase that leads to the bedroom, which overlooks the Golden Gate Bridge. Another guest room features a sunken bathtub large enough for two. Several rooms overlook the scrupulously tended garden. Each guest room contains antiques, books that you should have read, a complimentary carafe of sherry, and fresh flowers.

The complimentary breakfast is brought to your room on a tray set with Copeland, Spode, or Wedgwood china. At bedtime, look before you lie down: Whoever turns the beds down places fortune cookies on the pillows, and you might have to shake the crumbs out of your hair while reading a fortune like "The cistern contains, the fountain overflows."

Advance reservations are strongly recommended.

Accommodations: 8 rooms, 4 with private bath. *Smoking:* Permitted; *Children:* Over 12 permitted. *Pets:* Not permitted. *Breakfast:* Included. *Driving Instructions:* Take Court Street to Charlton Court, a half-block street.

Bock's Bed and Breakfast

1448 Willard Street, San Francisco, CA 94117. (415) 664-6842. *Host:* Laura J. Bock.

Bock's Bed and Breakfast is a 1906 Edwardian-style structure that was built immediately after the San Francisco earthquake. On a hill in the Parnassus Heights area (adjacent to Sutro Forest), the house has a spectacular view of San Francisco and the hills surrounding it. The front yard is full of flowering Japanese plum trees.

The living room, carpeted in a warm shade of green, has a piano and a pair of French doors that open onto a deck overlooking the city. Each guest room, carpeted wall-to-wall, features twin beds, fresh flowers, a small refrigerator, and an electric coffeepot. The dining room, where Laura serves a Continental breakfast (fresh juices and fruit in season, fresh rolls with English marmalade and jams, and coffee and tea), also affords a splendid view.

Laura, a free-lance business-services consultant, invites guests to share her garden, which has a patio and lawn furniture. The garden, which used to be quite a formal one, is frequented by Pokey McTavish, a Scottish terrier not at all undisposed to visitors.

Accommodations: 2 rooms, 1 with private bath. *Smoking:* Permitted. *Children:* Permitted. *Pets:* Not permitted. *Breakfast:* Included. *Driving Instructions:* Three blocks from Golden Gate Park.

San Francisco **CALIFORNIA**

Casa Arguello

2205 Arguello Street, San Francisco, CA 94118. (415) 752-9482. *Hostess:* Emma Baires.

Located a few blocks from the Golden Gate Bridge in the Presido Heights section of town, Casa Arguello is an extremely large apartment. At one time it was an annex for Lone Mountain College and Emma Baires had twenty-four coeds living with her. Mrs. Baires, obviously, loves company.

The apartment contains electrified wall sconces, chandeliers, French doors, curved windows, and antique furnishings. There are brass beds, gilded mirrors, heavily tufted chairs, numerous plants, and molded walls and ceilings.

Emma has a large living room, with a long couch covered in an elegant floral print fabric, two tufted chairs upholstered in beige, two other tufted chairs and a matching tufted love seat, and an antique coffee table usually bedecked with flowers.

The apartment has a two-room master suite on the main floor, as well as five bedrooms on the upper floor. The upstairs bedrooms overlook the gardens of surrounding homes.

Visitors from all over the world come to stay here, and one would be hard pressed to tell if they come for the elegance, the warmth, the convenience, or all three.

Accommodations: 5 rooms, 2 with private bath. *Smoking:* Permitted. *Children:* Under 7 not permitted. *Pets:* Not permitted. *Driving Instructions:* Arguello Street is in Presido Heights, three blocks from the Golden Gate Bridge.

San Francisco **CALIFORNIA**

Casita Blanca

330 Edgehill Way, San Francisco, CA 94127. (415) 564-9339. *Hostess:* Joan M. Bard.

Built about 1920, Casita Blanca is a small West Coast cottage that is completely separate from the main house and that has a location unique for San Francisco—it's on top of a hill that overlooks parts of the city and the bay (it has a view of the Golden Gate Bridge), and it's surrounded by hundred-year-old pine trees.

Essentially a large studio room, the cottage features a painted brick fireplace, an alcove with a small desk, a dining area, a completely equipped kitchen, and a private bathroom with shower only. The French prints on the walls, the hardwood floors, the wool rug, the painting over the fireplace and the leather couch in front of it, give the cottage the feeling of a sitting room.

Joan doesn't serve breakfast but does leave condiments around on a "take a little, leave a little" basis. Guests are greeted by Tinkerbelle, a white bull terrier who appears to be ferocious, but is "really a love and won't eat you up."

Accommodations: 1 room (cottage) with private bath. *Smoking:* Permitted. *Children:* Permitted if accompanied by only one adult. *Pets:* Not permitted. *Driving Instructions:* Take Kensington to Vasquez, which turns into Garcia and then Edgehill Way; take a sharp right hairpin turn at the top of Edgehill Way.

Inn on Castro

321 Castro Street, San Francisco, CA 94114. (415) 861-0321. *Host:* Joel Roman.

The Inn on Castro is a 1910 Victorian structure with buttressed eaves that follow the contours of the facade's bay windows. Inside one finds very little Victoriana because Joel Roman, a painter and interior designer, has filled the old house with sleek modern furnishings and appointments. A series of tufted chocolate-brown seating modules line the walls of the living room, which features a bold kilim rug, a chrome and brass table, track lighting, a fireplace with a mirrored mantel, lots of plants, and a large, lush painting by Joel.

Papier-mâché parrots, soft sculptures, paper umbrellas suspended from the ceiling, a white oval table encircled by chairs upholstered in white, modular rattan storage cases, a handmade patchwork quilt, coolie hats hanging from the ceiling, a white lacquer headboard with matching chests—touches like these suggest Joel's flamboyant yet elegant taste.

The lovely rooms are the more so for such appointments as fresh flowers and chocolates waiting on the pillows of turned-down beds. Joel serves a complimentary breakfast on hand-painted plates that, guests gradually notice, he rotates each day.

Accommodations: 5 rooms with shared baths. *Smoking:* Permitted in guest rooms only. *Children:* Not permitted. *Pets:* Not permitted. *Breakfast:* Included. *Driving Instructions:* The Inn on Castro is at the intersection of Castro, Market, and Seventeenth.

Jackson Court City Share

2198 Jackson Street, San Francisco, CA 94115. (415) 929-7670. *Hostess:* Kathy Odsather.

With part of the fortune they amassed while dabbling in the railroad business, the Calahan family built this red stone mansion in 1904. Two years later, as the great San Francisco earthquake of 1906 was shaking the city into pieces, a totem pole Mrs. Calahan picked up during an Alaskan cruise tipped over and knocked her Chinese servant unconscious. Abandoned by even the foggiest notion of what to do, Mrs. Calahan took tea in her bedroom, wondering, one imagines, how properly to sip tea in a trembling mansion. When her servant finally came to, she passed out.

Jackson Court is decorated with a dazzling and eclectic mixture of antiques and modern pieces. A sleek modern couch upholstered in white Haitian cotton, with a brass coffee table in front of it and a turquoise and gold Persian rug beneath it, faces the fireplace. A handmade patchwork quilt covers the brass bed to the right of the couch, and three colors of paint cover the walls and molding.

Each floor of Jackson Court has a kitchen where a complimentary Continental breakfast is served. In the afternoons, complimentary sherry flows in the parlor, which has exposed-beam ceilings and a fireplace with male and female heads in bas-relief.

There is a minimum stay of one week.

Accommodations: 10 rooms with private bath. *Smoking:* Permitted. *Children:* Not permitted. *Pets:* Not permitted. *Breakfast:* Included. *Driving Instructions:* In the heart of San Francisco.

Ole Rafael Bed and Breakfast

1629 Fifth Avenue, San Rafael, CA 94901. (415) 453-0414. *Hosts:* Timothy and Pat O'Shea.

Located next to San Rafael's Mansion Row, the Ole Rafael is an 1865 Gothic Revival house. The town, which grew around an old Roman Catholic mission, used to be a mecca for wealthy San Franciscans looking to escape the big city but to escape it in style. The town is rife with huge, opulent mansions.

The "wedding suite," which you needn't be newly married to occupy, has a brick fireplace, 14-foot ceilings, a beige antique satin bedspread, gold carpeting, and shuttered windows covered with green floral curtains that match the wallpaper. The dining room also has a fireplace, and a Louis XIV couch upholstered in a floral brocade dresses up the parlor.

Guests are served complimentary wine when they arrive. A complimentary breakfast brought to your room on French wicker trays always includes homemade breads, croissants or brioches, fresh fruit in season, juice, and coffee.

Accommodations: 4 rooms with shared baths. *Smoking:* Tolerated. *Children:* Over 1 year permitted. *Pets:* Small dogs permitted. *Breakfast:* Included. *Driving Instructions:* Take Route 101 to the San Rafael exit, follow signs to Mission Archangel, and make a left on Fifth Avenue.

The Blue Quail Inn

1908 Bath Street, Santa Barbara, CA 93101. (805) 687-2300. *Hostess:* Jeanise Suding.

Situated under a large oak tree, The Blue Quail Inn is an early-twentieth-century redwood frame house, with a secluded backyard complete with a picnic table and chairs. Jeanise used to be involved in the aerospace industry but exchanged the world of high tech for a bed-and-breakfast place in her hometown.

Jeanise offers guests two rooms in the main house and three other rooms in two nearby cottages. One of the cottages has a bedroom, a living room, a dining area, a kitchen, and a bath. All the rooms feature something special—one has bay windows with a comfortably upholstered window seat, another has a canopied bed with quilted pillows and a white comforter. Guests are invited to use the living room in the main house.

Each morning in the dining room Jeanise serves a complimentary Continental breakfast that usually includes juice, coffee, popovers, and bran muffins. Later in the evening, Jeanise is wont to share a brandy or some hot cider with her guests.

Accommodations: 5 rooms, 1 with private bath. *Smoking:* Permitted. *Children:* Permitted in one cottage only. *Pets:* Not permitted. *Driving Instructions:* From Route 101 South, take the Mission Street off-ramp and turn left; go two blocks and turn right onto Bath Street.

The Parsonage

1600 Olive Street, Santa Barbara, CA 93101. (805) 962-9336. *Hostess:* Hilda Michelmore.

Originally a Rectory for the Trinity Episcopal Church, the Parsonage is an 1892 Queen Anne Victorian structure painted tan and trimmed in blue. The building has a sun deck from which you can descry the ocean, as well as a front porch embellished with intricate woodwork.

The living room has a striking purple Oriental rug with a floral pattern in greens and roses at its corners, and fringes the color of wheat; a fireplace carved out of birds'-eye redwood; and windows that extend almost from floor to ceiling with hand-carved redwood moldings. The dining room features bay windows with birds'-eye redwood moldings and lace tieback curtains; a gray Oriental rug with blue trim and wheat-colored fringes, and a glass-doored hutch displaying Hilda's crystal-and-china collection.

One guest suite has a king-size canopied bed, a light blue Oriental rug with a beige, tan, and apricot design at its corners, a mahogany armoire with a mirror, and an antique brass chandelier with hand-blown fluted glass. The suite opens into the solarium, which features rattan furniture covered in a wheat-colored fabric, 180 degrees of windows, and a floor covered by a durrie rug from India. The bathroom has a pedestal sink, a claw-footed tub, and shower curtains that match the wallpaper.

Hilda used to own a Volkswagen dealership but got involved with a guest house because she loves to decorate and entertain. She does both well.

Accommodations: 4 rooms, 2 with private bath. *Smoking:* Permitted. *Children:* Permitted. *Pets:* Not permitted. *Breakfast:* Included. *Driving Instructions:* From Los Angeles take the Ventura Freeway and continue on Route 101 to Santa Barbara Street; turn right, go 1 mile to Arrellage Street, turn right again, and go four blocks to Olive Street.

Sunnyside, an Urban Inn

435 East McKinley Avenue, Sunnyvale, CA 94086. (408) 736-3794. *Hosts:* Byrd and Phyllis Helligas.

A 1930s Italianate peasant-style building with a stucco entrance on a low, broad frame, Sunnyside used to be a potato-chip factory. Byrd and Phyllis incorporated many remnants of the factory into decorative or functional pieces. The sculpture on the front lawn is its old stapling machine, and the glass-topped table in the atrium used to be the candy cooker.

Byrd and Phyllis bought Sunnyside in 1976 and have brought into it numerous pieces of urban archaelogy—the iron lamps with burlap covers that hang in the keeping room used to be San Jose streetlamps; the knob and tube light in the atrium was once a City of Santa Clara light; an old "account safe" is now a storage bin.

The house still has the old hydraulic freight elevator, which huffs and puffs its way from the basement to the second floor.

The guest rooms, which have private entrances, are furnished eclectically, with antiques and memorabilia setting the tone. One room has sliding glass doors that open into the atrium, and another features a kitchen area, as well as a hall dressing and sitting area. The patio, which guests are welcome to use, has a fireplace.

"Breakfast is served at the time and place of the guest's choice."

Accommodations: 2 rooms with private bath. *Smoking:* Permitted. *Children:* Permitted. *Pets:* Not permitted. *Breakfast:* Included. *Driving Instructions:* Take Route 101 south from San Francisco; exit at Mathilda Avenue; turn left on Washington, right on Bayview, and then left on McKinley.

The Bank Inn

6 Eureka Street, Sutter Creek, CA 95685. (209) 267-0398.
Hosts: Janelle, Mimi, and Michael Ford.

The Bank Inn was built in the late 1860s as a boardinghouse for miners. The saltbox structure has a downstairs room—with walls of river rock and iron bar windows—that maintains a 60-degree temperature year round. Rumor has it the room once served as one of Amador County's "unofficial" banks.

With the help of her mother, Mimi, and her brother, Michael, Janelle Ford completely refinished the former boardinghouse, furnishing it with country antiques and making sure the coffee pot is always on. One of the five guest rooms has a king-size brass bed and a private bath. The four other rooms, two with double beds and two with twins, share two baths. The parlor has a television set and a large assortment of books and magazines. The backyard, which overlooks Sutter Creek, has a grape arbor and plenty of outdoor furniture.

Janelle serves a full complimentary breakfast that includes farm-fresh eggs, homemade jams, sausage or bacon, coffee cake, and quiche or crepes. The latest projects around the property are a gazebo and a vegetable garden.

Accommodations: 5 rooms, 1 with private bath. *Smoking:* Permitted. *Children:* Permitted. *Pets:* Not permitted. *Breakfast:* Included. *Driving Instructions:* Take Route 49, which turns into Main Street in Sutter Creek; proceed to Eureka Street.

The Foxes in Sutter Creek

77 Main Street, P. O. Box 159 Sutter Creek, CA 95685. (209) 267-5882. *Hosts:* Pete and Min Fox.

The Foxes' 1857 New England–style house contains Pete Fox's real estate office, Min Fox's antique shop, the couple's private residence, and a guest suite with a private bath.

A 9-foot-tall Victorian headboard, entirely of walnut, and a matching tall dresser, with a white marble top at table level, dominate the bedroom, one of whose walls supports a 30- by 40-inch oil painting by John Orth, an American Impressionist much influenced by Murillo. Another wall features a 1797 Louis XVI tapestry woven in grays, pale pinks, and antique burgundies. A brass chandelier shaded with cranberry glass imported from France hangs from the bedroom's ceiling, and an auburn wall-to-wall carpet covers the floor. The sitting room is furnished with a Queen Anne love seat covered in fawn velvet, as well as two Louis XV side chairs.

A complimentary breakfast of fresh fruit juice, freshly baked breads, and coffee is brought to the guest suite's door on a Towle silver serving tray strewn with fresh flowers. Each evening the Foxes provide a complimentary carafe of wine or sherry.

Accommodations: 1 suite with private bath. *Smoking:* Tolerated. *Children:* Not permitted. *Pets:* Not permitted. *Breakfast:* Included. *Driving Instructions:* Take Route 49 into Sutter Creek, where it becomes Main Street.

Mayfield House

236 Grove Street, Tahoe City, CA 95730. (916) 583-1001.
Hosts: John and Marsha Twichell.

A stone-and-wood structure built in 1932 by a successful Lake Tahoe contractor, Mayfield House is marked by steep gables, a stone path that runs through the garden, and a convenient location: You can walk anyplace in Tahoe, and a shuttle bus stops yards away to take you where your feet can't.

The living room has a large stone fireplace flanked on either side by windows looking over the lawn, plus wood paneling, large buttressed pine beams on the ceiling, two love seats covered with a fabric of blue and gray, and a dark brown plush carpet.

All of the Mayfield House guest rooms have down com-

forters; one has a sitting area with a view of the lake (a few hundred yards from the house), and another features a network of eaves covered in a tiny-print Victorian wallpaper.

Host John Twichell used to be the head of Lake Placid's Chamber of Commerce, and he and Marsha together have managed several ski lodges. They know how to make people comfortable. While light classical music plays in the background, they serve a complimentary breakfast of fresh orange juice, fresh fruit, coffee, and homemade pastries.

Accommodations: 6 rooms sharing 3 baths. *Smoking:* Permitted if smoker is considerate. *Children:* Over 12 permitted. *Pets:* Not permitted. *Breakfast:* Included. *Driving Instructions:* From Truckee, take Route 89 South; turn left at Grove Street.

Truckee **CALIFORNIA**

The Bradley House

P.O. Box 2011, Truckee, CA 95734. (916) 587-5388. *Hosts:* Donna and Larry Bradley.

This 1880 Victorian structure, its decorative trim painted gray and white, was built by a man who exported ice taken from a nearby river. The house has been lovingly restored by Donna and Larry Bradley, who have furnished it with their extensive collection of antiques.

The parlor has a Franklin stove, and a 9-foot oak and stained-glass back bar that, a hundred years or so ago, refreshed the guests of a Kansas City hotel. Hand-carved oak beds with hand-made Amish quilts appear in most of the guest rooms. Period reproduction wallpapers, chosen to complement the quilts, cover the guest-room walls. Most of the furnishings are antiques, and most are made of golden oak—even the toilet seats, the towel racks, and the toilet-tissue holders.

The Bradley House features such other niceties as a staircase with a carved banister and leather wainscoting; a large, rare rolltop table; several wood and glass display cabinets housing Larry's collection of ceramic figurine liquor decanters; and a color television set with cable and a video-recorder complete with several movies on tape.

The Bradleys serve a complimentary breakfast that includes—depending on whether Donna or Larry bake—homemade strudel or blueberry muffins. Each evening between 5 and 6, guests are offered complimentary wine and cheese.

Accommodations: 5 rooms with shared baths. *Smoking:* Not permitted. *Children:* Not permitted. *Pets:* Not permitted. *Breakfast:* Included. *Driving Instructions:* Take Route I-80 to the Central Truckee exit; follow Donner Pass Road into town; take Spring Street up the hill.

West Covina **CALIFORNIA**

The Hendrick Inn

2124 East Merced Avenue, West Covina, CA 91791. (213) 919-2125. *Hosts:* George and Mary Hendrick.

A U-shaped ranch-style house with a large deck overlooking a 20- by 40-foot swimming pool, the Hendrick Inn is full of decorative and creature-comfort surprises. The house was photographed, inside and out, for *Life* magazine. The deck, carpeted and done in rattan furniture upholstered in duck, has a Jacuzzi that holds six people.

One of the living rooms has a white marble fireplace, European reproductions of paintings by Velázquez, El Greco, and Van Gogh, a beige carpet that matches the color of the fireplace, and fabrics blended predominantly of cool colors—blues, greens, and lavenders. The other living room is suffused with warm colors and features a white brick fireplace.

The master suite, which has sliding glass doors that open onto the deck, has a walnut secretary with glass doors, a walnut chair upholstered in a beige, olive green, and blue fabric, and a teak-paneled wall. One guest room is done entirely in rainbow motifs, which are reflected in everything from the towels to the bedspread, and furnished in French provincial style. Mary and George's decorative eclecticism reaches its height in the "booze bath," which is wallpapered with more than three thousand labels removed from foreign liquor bottles.

Mary and George serve complimentary wine to their guests, as well as a complimentary liqueur on the first night of their stay. For an irresistibly reasonable price, they will serve guests a hard-to-forget dinner.

Accommodations: 4 rooms, 1 with private bath. *Smoking:* Permitted. *Children:* Permitted. *Pets:* Not permitted. *Driving Instructions:* From Los Angeles Take Route I-10 to West Covina, pick up Citrus Avenue and follow south to East Merced Avenue.

Burgundy House Country Inn

6711 Washington Street, Yountville, CA 94599. (707) 944-2855. *Hosts:* Mary and Robert Kennan.

The Burgundy House is an 1872 brandy distillery with 22-inch-thick fieldstone walls. Mary Kennan won an Award of Merit for its restoration. Her husband, Robert, an architect, designed and built an annex called the Bordeaux House—a formal red-brick structure all but hidden behind two old Italian stone pines.

The Burgundy House, convenient to some 120 Napa Valley wineries, is decorated with the antiques that Mary and Robert have accumulated over the years. The Bordeaux House, also furnished with antiques, mostly French country, has a fireplace in every room; each room also has a private patio. There are antique brass beds, colorful comforters, and decanted complimentary wine and glasses on the bureaus. Each guest room is air-conditioned.

Around the huge hearth in one of the Burgundy House's common rooms, Mary and Robert serve a complimentary breakfast; in the late afternoon, and sometimes into the evening, they offer complimentary wine.

Accommodations: 16 rooms, 11 with private bath. *Smoking:* Permitted. *Children:* Permitted in cottages. *Pets:* Not permitted. *Breakfast:* Included. *Driving Instructions:* From Napa, go north on Route 29 to Yountville; turn right on Madison Street; turn right on Washington Street.

Berthod. Berthod is the gateway to Rocky Mountain National Park, and the host here is a backpacking enthusiast who knows the park's trails well and is willing to take guests on tours. Also willing to cook meals for guests, he has a herb garden and an organic vegetable garden. The house is a turn-of-the-century brick structure on 2.5 acres of grounds. Its interior is notable for a great deal of woodwork. *Represented by:* Bed & Breakfast Colorado, (303) 333-3340. $20–$32.

Beulah. Part of a 67-acre working horse ranch, this four-bedroom home has sweeping views of mountains, two creeks running through the property, and a neighboring 600-acre park. The host enjoys restoring antique carriages and welcomes children and dogs. *Represented by:* Bed & Breakfast Colorado, (303) 333-3340. $20–$30.

Boulder. Hosted by a nature-loving hiker and marathon runner, this guest house features a bay-window area with wicker rockers, as well as an antique oaken fireplace. Almost all of the houses furnishings are of oak, including the desk in the guest bedroom. Breakfast is served in the country kitchen or on the guest's private patio. *Represented by:* Bed & Breakfast Colorado, (303) 333-3340. $25–$35.

Denver. Situated on 2.5 acres, this private cottage overlooks a pond with ducks, and every now and then an old horse wanders past. The hosts provide all the fixings for breakfast, which guests prepare themselves in the cottage's kitchen. Simply but comfortably furnished, the cottage has a living room, a private bath, and a convenient south-Denver location. *Represented by:* Bed & Breakfast Colorado, (303) 333-3340. $30–$40.

Denver. This ninth floor condominium which includes a king-size bed and a private bath, is in a building with tennis courts, an indoor swimming pool, a Jacuzzi, and racquetball courts. The apartment has spectacular views of Denver and the nearby mountains, especially from the balcony, which is furnished in white wicker. *Represented by:* Bed & Breakfast Colorado, (303) 333-3340. $30–$40.

Denver. The host, a former big-band vocalist, has a private basement apartment for guests. The apartment, in the eastern part of Denver, has a bedroom, sitting room, kitchen, and cable television set. Guests are invited to use the large above-ground pool and the laundry facilities. *Represented by:* Bed & Breakfast Colorado, (303) 333-3340. $20–$30.

Eaton. Situated at the planting line of a large farm, this ranch-style house is hosted by people interested in railroads, the Southwest's Indians, computers, and bridge. The living room has a fireplace, as well as windows with mountain views. There are bicycles for guests who request them, and the hosts are willing to cook meals for guests. *Represented by:* Bed & Breakfast Colorado, (303) 333-3340. $20–$28.

Lookout Mountain. Surrounded by evergreen trees, this guest cabin is on a hill that overlooks Denver. The cabin has a private bath and a kitchen, and the hosts, in the process of restoring a late-nineteenth-century house on the property, enjoy skiing and gardening. *Represented by:* Bed & Breakfast Colorado, (303) 333-3340. $25–$35.

Outlook Lodge

P.O. Box 5, Green Mountain Falls, CO 80819. (303) 684-2303. *Hosts:* The Ahern Family.

Originally built in 1889 as a summer parsonage for a church, the Outlook Lodge is a large Victorian structure with a wide veranda running across the better part of its front. Green Mountain Falls was a stopping place on the Old Ute Indian Trail. The Utes, after a season of hunting in what is now western Colorado, used to cross the Rockies at this point, stopping for a while to cure their sick and wounded in the hot springs now called Manitou Springs. "Manitou" is the Ute name for God, Whom they thought dwelled there.

The house, furnished with Victorian country antiques, features a large, sun-filled dining room (complete with a piano, games, toys, and an elaborate 1860s base-burner wood stove) that runs across one entire side. The small parlor has a fireplace and an antique desk, which Impy Ahern considers the perfect place for writing letters or cards. The large parlor has a color television set with Home Box Office.

The lodge features picnic and barbecue facilities in a forested area behind it; the view includes mountains and a small village.

The Aherns offer a complimentary breakfast and will put together a pack lunch for hikers, fishermen, or explorers.

Accommodations: 9 rooms, 2 with private bath. *Smoking:* Permitted. *Children:* Permitted. *Pets:* Permitted. *Breakfast:* Included. *Driving Instructions:* Green Mountain Falls is 15 miles west of Colorado Springs on Route 24 West.

Ouray **COLORADO**

Baker's Manor Guest House

317 Second Street, Ouray, CO 81427. (303) 325-4574. *Hosts:* John and Nancy Nixon.

Baker's Manor Guest House is a Victorian structure painted yellow with white trim. It was built in 1881, when local mines were active, but was deserted suddenly and remained empty until the 1950s. A woman named Mrs. Baker took over the property and turned it into a boardinghouse. Situated at an elevation of 8,000 feet, the building, which has landscaped grounds rife with wildflowers, has views of the San Juan Mountains.

Nancy, who runs a nursery school, and John, an architect, restored the house, furnishing it with some antiques and a collection of heirloom furniture. The guest rooms, four of which offer views of the mountains, contain such items as oaken dressers, iron beds, Oriental rugs, and an antique oaken armoire. The living room has a brick-and-tile fireplace and an antique couch upholstered in red velvet, and the halls are lined with family photographs, old and new, in antique frames.

Nancy and John serve a Continental breakfast that includes freshly baked breads. This guest house is open June 1 through October 1.

Accommodations: 6 rooms with shared bath. *Smoking:* Permitted. *Children:* Permitted. *Pets:* Not permitted. *Breakfast:* Included. *Driving Instructions:* From Montrose go 35 miles south of U.S. 550; Baker's Manor is a block west of Ouray's Main Street, between Second and Third avenues.

Nederland **COLORADO**

Goldminer Hotel

Eldora Star Route, Nederland, CO 80466. (303) 258-7770.
Hosts: Dwight and Jean Dell.

An 1897 log building, the Goldminer Hotel has something of a Dodge City facade. "Originally, the rooms were rented in eight-hour shifts, but a bullet hole in one of the doors attests to someone's desire for a longer snooze," explains Dwight. As far as its grounds are concerned, suffice it to say the Goldminer is located in the Roosevelt National Forest, not far from the Continental Divide.

All of the guest rooms, furnished with antiques, have views of the surrounding mountains; one room features five large windows overlooking the Indian Peaks Wilderness Area.

The lobby, where the guests usually congregate, has a wood-burning stove that helps take the edge off the cold (the elevation here exceeds 9,000 feet). Dwight and Jean serve a complimentary breakfast each morning.

The Eldora area is rife with streams, lakes, and waterfalls. The Eldora Ski Area is 3 miles from the Goldminer, and cross-country skiing is even closer.

Accommodations: 5 rooms with shared baths. *Smoking:* Not permitted. *Children:* Permitted. *Pets:* Not permitted. *Driving Instructions:* The Goldminer is 3 miles west of Nederland, in the townsite of Eldora.

Groton Long Point **CONNECTICUT**

Shore Inne

54 East Shore Road, Groton Long Point, CT 06340. (203) 536-1180. *Hostess:* Helen Ellison.

A *circa*-1915 Colonial-style structure, the Shore Inne was built by a couple who used to live next door to it. Show-business people, the couple, so the story goes, built the Shore Inne to accommodate an overflow of guests. Even though the current zoning laws prohibit inns in this area, the Shore Inne exists because of a "grandfather clause," which basically says, "What's already here can stay."

The house is on the shore of the Long Island Sound, and the living room, dining room, and sun parlor all have views of the water. The living room is furnished with white wicker, with cushions covered in a yellow, green, and bittersweet floral fabric. The sun parlor, also a library, features television and hand-stenciled walls. The dining room features a maple hutch and a china cupboard. Of the seven guest rooms, six have views of the water and all have patchwork coverlets.

The Shore Inne's location is eminently convenient: Mystic is 3.5 miles away, Groton 8 miles, and New London 10 miles. The area features, as well as its natural beauty, plenty of restaurants and other attractions.

Accommodations: 7 rooms, 3 with private bath. *Smoking:* Permitted. *Children:* Permitted. *Pets:* Not permitted. *Breakfast:* Included. *Driving Instructions:* Take I-95 to exit 88, follow Route 1 to Route 215, turn onto Groton Long Point Road, and take the first left after the Yankee Fisherman Restaurant.

1833 House

33 Greenmanville Avenue (Route 27), Mystic, CT 06355. (203) 572-0633. *Hostess:* Joan Brownell Smith.

1833 House was erected in the year of its name, probably by someone involved in the construction of whaling vessels, which was a thriving industry in Mystic 150 years ago. The house is right next door to the Mystic Seaport Museum.

The living room, originally the kitchen, has hardwood floors, a Victorian love seat upholstered in pink brocade, a dark-wood lady's writing desk, and other comfortable furniture.

Two guest accommodations have views of Mystic Seaport, another consists of two bedrooms and serves as something of a family unit: The children's room, which has attached white beds, adjoins the parents' bedroom, which has a painted pine double bed, an antique blanket chest with a television set on top of it, and a private bath.

Joan used to work at the local tourists' information center and, consequently, knows a great deal about the area. She's willing to pick up guests at the Amtrak station.

Joan serves a Continental breakfast with a choice of three kinds of juice, muffins with jam, and coffee.

Accommodations: 4 rooms, 2 with private bath. *Smoking:* Permitted. *Children:* Permitted. *Pets:* Permitted. *Breakfast:* Included. *Driving Instructions:* From I-95 take exit 90 and go 1 mile south, just past the south entrance to the Mystic Seaport Museum.

Georgetown. This Victorian townhouse in the heart of Georgetown is hosted by a couple who run their own business and who speak Spanish, Portuguese, and Italian, as well as English. The house is comfortably furnished, and public transportation is half a block away. *Represented by:* Sweet Dreams & Toast, (202) 363-4712. $35.

Northwestern Washington. Filled with objects d'art collected during the hosts' extensive travels, each of the rooms in this guest house has a motif: There are a Chinese room, a Victorian room, and so forth. The house, just off the Rock Creek Parkway, has five bedrooms, four baths, and a wooded area behind it. *Represented by:* Sweet Dreams & Toast, (202) 363-4712. $50.

Dupont Circle. This split-level apartment in the heart of Washington has a first-floor picture window that overlooks Dupont Circle, as well as a small patio area that guests are invited to use. *Represented by:* Sweet Dreams & Toast, (202) 363-4712. $50.

Chevy Chase, D.C. A building dating from the early 1900s, this guest house has French doors in the living room and dining room, a fireplace surrounded by built-in bookcases, and a study that also contains built-in bookcases. *Represented by:* Sweet Dreams & Toast, (202) 363-4712. $40.

American University Area. Half a block from a bus stop, this accommodation is in a condominium building with round-the-clock security. *Represented by:* The Bed & Breakfast League, Ltd., 17 Northwest, 232-8718. $30–$38.

Chevy Chase Circle. Near Connecticut Avenue and only one block from a bus stop, this accommodation is 20 minutes from downtown Washington and has air conditioning and television. It is also close to shops and restaurants. *Represented by:* The Bed & Breakfast League, Ltd., 20 Upper Northwest, (202) 232-8718. $30–$38.

South Capitol Hill. Ten minutes from an airport and half a block from a bus stop, this Capitol Hill accommodation offers racket-club and swimming facilities, which guests may use for a fee. *Represented by:* The Bed & Breakfast League, Ltd., 28 Southeast, (202) 232-8718. $30–$38.

Amelia Island. Situated directly on the Atlantic, this family-owned guest house has six guest suites with living room and bedroom areas. For those who like heights, the hosts offer guests a suite at the top of a lighthouse. Breakfast includes hot breads and muffins. *Represented by:* Sun Coast Accommodations in Florida, (813) 393-7020. $55–$70.

Apollo Beach. This contemporary home has a golf course in front of it and a canal behind it. The house has its own dock, and the host has a boat on which he's willing to take guests out. (He knows the best fishing holes in Florida.) Guests have a choice between a room with a private bath and one with a shared bath. Continental breakfast is served. *Represented by:* Sun Coast Accommodations in Florida, (813) 393-7020. $30.

Boynton Beach. This guest house in a quiet neighborhood has a swimming pool and a separate entrance for guests. The host, who conducts painting classes, has a pottery studio behind his house. *Represented by:* Bed & Breakfast of the Palm Beaches, (305) 746-2545. $30.

Cape Kennedy. Involved in public relations and real estate (and, therefore, a Cape Kennedy booster), the host here gives guests a complimentary box of grapefruits or oranges, as well as a poster commemorating the first moon walk. This one-story home has two rooms for guests. *Represented by:* Sun Coast Accommodations in Florida, (813) 393-7020. $30.

Gainesville. The hosts—who speak Finnish and Portuguese, as well as English—have three bedrooms available for guests. The house, located in a college town, features lawns, lounge chairs, and a patio area. You may be able to cajole the hosts into taking you on a tour of the area. *Represented by:* Sun Coast Accommodations in Florida, (813) 393-7020. $30.

Hudson. This rambling modern home on 6 acres of land features exposed brick walls, a large pool and bathhouse, and plenty of open space. The hosts, one in real estate and the other a private nurse, have horses that roam about their veldtlike property. Lodging here is available only by the week. *Represented by:* Sun Coast Accommodations, (813) 393-7020. $450–$500.

Hypoluxo. Surrounded by fruit trees and filled with heirloom antiques and bric-a-brac such as glass figurine bottles, this guest house has a separate entrance for guests and also a private dock. *Represented by:* Bed & Breakfast of the Palm Beaches, (305) 746-2545. $35.

Jupiter. The host, retired from the lumber business, has a modern ranch-style house directly on an inlet, 150 feet from the ocean. He offers a pool, a fireplace, and excellent opportunities to fish for snook in the inlet. There are tennis courts next door to the house. *Represented by:* Bed & Breakfast of the Palm Beaches, (305) 746-2545. $50.

Jupiter. This guest house is furnished with antiques such as a rosewood piano and a walnut desk from the host's grandfather's hardware store in Tennessee. The house has a pool, and every bed is covered by a handmade quilt. Homemade sourdough English muffins are part of the breakfast. *Represented by:* Bed & Breakfast of the Palm Beaches, (305) 746-2545. $35–$45.

Jupiter West. An Englishwoman devoted to the bed-and-breakfast concept, the hostess has a ranch-style house on several acres of grounds. She also has a riding stable and quite a few horses. *Represented by:* Bed & Breakfast of the Palm Beaches, (305) 746-2545. $35.

Key West. This small Victorian house with gingerbread trim has six bedrooms with private baths available for guests. Owned by two gentlemen, the house is surrounded by lush tropical gardens and is furnished casually, primarily in wicker. *Represented by:* Sun Coast Accommodations in Florida, (813) 393-7020. $45–$55.

New Port Richey. A white two-story brick structure, this guest house, on a country road and surrounded by generous amounts of undeveloped land, is hosted by a retired couple willing to lend the guests bicycles and fishing rods. The guest rooms have private baths and television. The decor—typified by wicker furniture and a yellow, lime green, and white color scheme—lends the place a summery feeling. *Represented by:* Sun Coast Accommodations in Florida, (813) 393-7020. $45.

Pompano Beach. A brick house that features a whirlpool bath, this accommodation is hosted by someone with a green thumb. Antique bowls filled with freshly cut flowers appear all over the house, which is furnished in Oriental motifs. The host has a greenhouse, where he grows orchids and African violets, and the house has a patio. *Represented by:* Bed & Breakfast of the

Palm Beaches, (305) 746-2545. $35–$45.

Saint Augustine. This restored Spanish-style house in the historic St. George area has five rooms available for guests. A buffet breakfast is served in a large meeting room with a fireplace. The hosts give honeymooners a complimentary bottle of champagne and bowl of fruit. *Represented by:* Sun Coast Accommodations in Florida, (813) 393-7020. $35–$45.

Seminole. One of the hosts is a member of the local industrial council, and the other is an avid kayaker, canoer, and whitewater rafter willing to take guests on outings. The house is furnished with a combination of contemporary and early-American furniture, and the hosts speak Swedish and Norwegian, as well as English. For a small fee, guests may use the hosts' beach club facilities. *Represented by:* Sun Coast Accommodations in Florida, (813) 393-7020. $30–$35.

Stuart. Five miles from the ocean, this guest house has a sun deck, a hot tub, and a private pond stocked with fish. The living room contains a stone fireplace and a host of metalwork decorations, especially eagles. *Represented by:* Bed & Breakfast of the Palm Beaches, (305) 746-2545. $35–$50.

Tampa. The hosts—involved in real estate, investments, and a temporary-help agency—have three guest rooms in their brick contemporary home on a corner lot. A pool, sauna, and private beach are available to guests. The house is furnished with sleek modern pieces (a mirrored wall in the den is representative of the decor). The hosts often prepare guests' meals, for an extra charge. *Represented by:* Sun Coast Accommodations in Florida, (813) 393-7020. $35.

Tampa. The two guest rooms here share a bath, but each has its own television set. This modern apartment is in a country-club area that offers a swimming pool, tennis and racquetball courts, and other recreational facilities. The apartment has a terrace. *Represented by:* Sun Coast Accommodations in Florida, (813) 393-7020. $35.

Tampa. Overlooking the bay and with biking and jogging trails right outside its door, this Victorian house contains antique furnishings such as four-poster beds. An extensive antique-doll collection is housed in a small upstairs anteroom. Other features include a large foyer and reception room, wide-paneled wooden floors, and two upstairs bedrooms with fine views. *Represented by:* Sun Coast Accommodations in Florida, (813) 393-7020. $30–$35.

Treasure Island. You can take the elevator to the sand: This one-bedroom condominium is directly on the ocean, which it faces. The apartment, furnished eclectically, is in a building that has a large lounge area surrounding a swimming pool, which guests are invited to use. The host, who teaches French, gives guests the run of the apartment, including kitchen privileges. *Represented by:* Sun Coast Accommodations in Florida, (813) 393-7020. $45.

West Palm Beach. From the balcony of this eighth-floor apartment you can look across Lake Worth and see Palm Beach. The building has a pool, a sauna, tennis courts, and exercise rooms, and there is a white-sand lakeside beach. *Represented by:* Bed & Breakfast of the Palm Beaches, (305) 746-2545. $40.

West Palm Beach. This guest house on the shore of a lake in the heart of West Palm Beach has a pool and a large screened-in patio. The host extends kitchen privileges to guests. *Represented by:* Bed & Breakfast of the Palm Beaches, (305) 746-2545. $30.

The Livery Stable

100 Ring Avenue, Tarpon Springs, FL 33589. (813) 938-5547. *Hosts:* Marvin and Ingrid Jones.

Built around the turn of the century out of hand-hewn concrete blocks, The Livery Stable originally functioned as a livery stable, but the advent of the automobile eliminated the need for a large livery stable in Tarpon Springs. The horse and mule stalls were converted into a lobby, and the building turned into a boardinghouse that catered primarily to the Greek fishermen who worked in the sponge-gathering industry.

Most guest rooms face south and even in winter admit plenty of Florida sunshine. Large and high-ceilinged, the guest rooms are simply but comfortably furnished and feature cable television sets.

The Livery Stable has for the guests' use a living room, dining room, and kitchen. The Joneses serve approximately three evening meals per week as well as a complimentary breakfast.

Close to the Gulf of Mexico, The Livery Stable is five minutes away from white sand beaches, golf courses, tennis courts, and picnic facilities. Horse and greyhound racing takes place the year round, and deep-sea boats sail daily from local docks.

Accommodations: 12 rooms with shared baths. *Smoking:* Permitted. *Children:* Permitted except in winter. *Pets:* Permitted if small. *Breakfast:* Included. *Driving Instructions:* In the center of downtown Tarpon Springs.

Historic Area. A renovated early-1900s home in a designated historic area, this guest house features a room with a queen-size bed, a large sitting area, and an adjoining bath. The house has a large deck and a backyard swimming pool. Hosted by a corporate executive and a nurse, this accommodation is two blocks from Atlanta's Cultural Art Center, which has a museum and a theater, where the Atlanta Symphony plays. *Represented by:* Bed & Breakfast Atlanta, (404) 378-6026. $32–$36.

Druid Hills. Designed by a leading architect, this Georgian-style house is in Druid Hills, a designated historic area. A broad staircase leads from the entrance hall to the second-floor guest room, which has a frilly canopied bed, as well as an adjoining bath with floor-to-ceiling tiles. Guests are invited to enjoy the semi-formal garden, the living room, the dining room, and the library. *Represented by:* Bed & Breakfast Atlanta, (404) 378-6026. $36–$40.

Morningside Area. A retired educator with a vast knowledge of Atlanta and environs hosts this well-maintained old home in one of Atlanta's more convenient suburbs. A room with twin beds and a private bath is available for guests. The house is close to public transportation. *Represented by:* Bed & Breakfast Atlanta, (404) 378-6026. $28–$32.

Atlanta Northwest. A late-nineteenth-century Victorian structure, this guest house is hosted by a medical doctor and a doctor of musicology. They offer guests two bedrooms, each with a private bath. The location has excellent expressway connections to all local points of interest. *Represented by:* Bed & Breakfast Atlanta, (404) 378-6026. $36–$40.

The De Loffre House

812 Broadway, Columbus, GA 31901. (404) 324-1144.
Hosts: Shirley and Paul Romo.

Once inhabited by a steamship baron who claimed to be directly descended from William the Conqueror, this 1883 Italianate town house is on the brick-paved parkway that runs through Columbus's Historic District.

The De Loffre House has been thoroughly restored and modernized—its antique furnishings and modern conveniences ride comfortably at anchor. Each guest room has a fireplace, a private bath, a color television set, and toilet accessories for those who forget their own. No one forgets Shirley and Paul's complimentary breakfast, which is served on antique china with candles burning on the tables.

Some guest rooms have four-poster beds, some have carved spool beds, some have chandeliers, some have Oriental and Persian rugs. In each, a complimentary bottle of sherry and a bowl of fruit are set out.

Accommodations: 4 rooms with private bath. *Smoking:* Permitted. *Children:* Permitted. *Pets:* Not permitted. *Breakfast:* Included. *Driving Instructions:* Take Route 280 into Columbus (the house is four blocks from the highway).

Savannah **GEORGIA**

Eliza Thompson House

5 West Jones Street, Savannah, GA 31401. (912) 355-0541 or (912) 236-7913. *Hostess:* Tana Mitchell.

This town house was built in 1847 for Miss Eliza, a pretty redhead with seven children who, on her kitchen's large hearth, baked corn cakes to sell to General Sherman's soldiers. One legend has it that Sherman didn't destroy Savannah because he couldn't resist Miss Eliza's corn cakes.

Interested in preserving the past, owners Jim and Laurie Widman see to it that breakfast includes Miss Eliza's corn cakes, the recipe for which they still follow. The past reappeared recently during an elaborate restoration undertaken by the Widmans. Breaking through a wall of an upstairs bathroom, they discovered a fireplace; in the living room they found a handhewn, 2-foot-square and 20-foot-long oak log, which they decided to leave exposed—albeit cleaned up—over the windows; and after scraping away paint and wallpaper, they uncovered 20-inch-wide clear cedar paneling over the fireplaces in the parlor and the foyer.

The inn features an enclosed private courtyard, a garden with an 8-foot-high copper sculpture and a fountain. Fireplaces, heart pine floors, Oriental rugs, and a large collection of Vanity Fair prints suggest the Widmans' taste.

Guests are welcomed with a glass of complimentary sherry, and later in the evening they frequently gather around the bar, where they mix their own drinks.

Accommodations: 17 rooms with private bath. *Smoking:* Permitted. *Children:* Under 10 not permitted. *Pets:* Not permitted. *Breakfast:* Included. *Driving Instructions:* Take Liberty Street to Whittaker and make a right; then turn left on West Jones Street.

The Halsam-Fort House

417 East Charlton Street, Savannah, GA 31401. (912) 233-6380. *Host:* Alan Fort.

Every so often, late in the evening, the ghost of its original owner stomps around on the third floor of the Halsam-Fort House. A minstrel show impresario unfortunately lynched by an irate Ohio audience for whom he failed to produce a show, John Halsam left behind him an 1872 brick Italianate home. It's now a landmark building, as well as a bed-and-breakfast inn, in the middle of Savannah's Historic District.

Alan Fort, the current owner, lives on the top two floors—with the ghost, many antiques (he has an interest in an antique business), and an extensive collection of antique dolls and toys. The entire garden level is a guest accommodation. With a living room, two bedrooms, a full bath, and a "country kitchen," the guest suite can accommodate one or two couples or a medium-sized family. Mr Fort never asks strangers to share the suite.

The living room has a Savannah-gray brick fireplace; an 1840 Pennsylvania pine apothecary cabinet; two wing chairs covered and quilted in a light navy blue broadcloth with bird and flower patterns in beiges, whites, and yellows; and a view through two windows of the English Regency Townhouses across the street.

One bedroom has twin brass beds and a fireplace, another has a double bed and oaken Victorian furnishings. For parties of guests that require more sleeping room, the sofa in the living room is a convertible with a queen-size mattress.

Although Mr. Fort doesn't prepare breakfast, the suite's kitchen has plenty of cookware, a dinner service and flatware for eight, a coffee maker, and a refrigerator stocked with soft drinks.

Mr. Fort, who traditionally invites guests for a tour of his home and a small libation of an evening, reports that his average guest tends to be an "explorer kind of person."

Accommodations: 1 suite with private bath. *Smoking:* Permitted. *Children:* Permitted. *Pets:* Permitted but with a charge. *Driving Instructions:* Between Habersham and Price streets, just off Troup Square, in the Historic District.

Liberty Inn, 1834

128 West Liberty Street, Savannah, GA 31401. (912) 233-1007. *Hosts:* Janie and Frank Harris.

The Liberty Inn was built in 1834 by a militia colonel named William Thorne Williams. The colonel was also a bookseller, a publisher, and a six-term mayor of Savannah. Constructed of bricks overlaid with clapboard, the Federal-style building survived the numerous fires that devastated early Savannah.

Somewhere in the middle of reconstructing the house, Frank Harris, nervously perusing estimates that had quadrupled, thought there was no way he could afford that much house. So he and his wife, Janie, both of whom operate restaurants in Savannah, decided to open their doors to guests, which they had thought about doing anyway.

The Harrises have four guest suites, two of them with three rooms. Each suite has a private entrance, individually controlled air conditioning, a telephone, a color television with Home Box Office, laundry facilities, and a complete kitchen. Although they no longer function—which perhaps explains why the house escaped so many fires—earthen-fired brick fireplaces appear in all but one suite.

Exposed ceiling-beams are found throughout the house, and the landscaped courtyard, with fruit trees and a grape arbor, features a solar spa with a whirlpool bath (great except in the winter—"last year we had two inches of ice on it"). For those not in the mood to take advantage of their suite's kitchen, the Harrises serve a complimentary breakfast of orange juice, coffee, and Danish.

Accommodations: 6 rooms with private bath. *Smoking:* Permitted. *Children:* Permitted. *Pets:* Not permitted. *Breakfast:* Included. *Driving Instructions:* Take Route 1-16 to Ogelthorpe Avenue; turn south and go one block on Barnard Street to Liberty Street.

Savannah **GEORGIA**

Mary Lee Guest Accommodations

117 East Jones Street, Savannah, GA. *Mailing Address:* P.O. Box 607, Savannah, GA 31402. (912) 232-0891. *Hostess:* Mary Lee.

"They seem to feel my presence even though I'm not visible," says Mary Lee of her guests. The presence they feel wanders around among old iron beds, handmade quilts, a wicker immigrant's trunk from Bulgaria, fresh flowers, afghans, exposed beams, fireplaces, and bowls of fruit.

This 1854 tabby-over-brick Savannah town house has a courtyard—complete with a bougainvillea-covered statue of Saint Francis—that is totally enclosed by a foot-thick wall of Savannah-Gray brick. The carriage house at one end of the courtyard contains two of Mary Lee's three guest suites. Each suite has a living room, a bedroom, and a kitchen, which Mary stocks with coffee, juice, and fresh fruit. The suites have telephones and central air conditioning.

Mary Lee always keeps a bottle of cold champagne around in case some honeymooners show up, or a couple celebrating an anniversary comes, or if it turns out to be a guest's birthday.

Accommodations: 3 apartments with private baths. *Smoking:* Permitted. *Children:* Permitted. *Pets:* Not permitted. *Breakfast:* Food for preparation by guests included. *Driving Instructions:* Take I-16 into Savannah; turn right on Liberty; turn right on Abercorn; then right on Jones Street.

Remshart-Brooks House

106 Jones Street West, Savannah, GA 31401. (912) 236-4337. *Hosts:* Martha and Charles Brooks.

In 1854, Mr. Remshart built Remshart's Row—a series of four red-brick Savannah town houses. He had three sons and one daughter—hence, the four units, Martha Brooks explains.

Martha and Charles Brooks have one guest-accommodation—a garden suite with a bedroom, a living and dining room, and a full kitchen. The bedroom has a four-poster bed, shuttered windows, many green plants, and a working fireplace. The living room also has a fireplace (which is unusually large because this room originally served as a kitchen), late-nineteenth-century furnishings, paintings by local artists, and a sofa that opens into a double bed. The living room also has a color television set with cable, and a library offering everything from Nancy Drew and the Hardy Boys to tomes on Savannah history.

The guest suite has two private entrances, one of which opens onto a walled courtyard, which Martha recommends for afternoon coffee or cocktails.

The Brookses consider sharing their home with guests "one of life's extras." Their rates include a complimentary Continental breakfast.

Accommodations: 1 apartment with private bath. *Smoking:* Permitted. *Children:* Permitted. *Pets:* Not Permitted. *Breakfast:* Food for preparation by guests included. *Driving Instructions:* Take Route I-95 to Route I-16; take exit 37B. Make a right turn at the first traffic light, a right at the next traffic light (Whitaker Street), and a right on Jones Street West.

Hawaii. On a cliff overlooking Hilo Bay and the Pacific, this guest accommodation has a private entrance and a shaded lanai. Twenty minutes from the airport. *Represented by:* Bed & Breakfast Hawaii, H-1A, (808) 822-1582. $25–$28.

Hawaii. On landscaped property in the hilly area of Hilo, this A-frame home offers two bedrooms to guests. Close to the airport and near the ocean, this accommodation is convenient to beaches and parks. *Represented by:* Bed & Breakfast Hawaii, H-2, (808) 822-1582. $19–$24.

Hawaii. Near Boiling Pots, a Hilo attraction, this designer home enjoys a view of Mauna Kea and the ocean. The host, who knows the island well, frequently acts as a tour guide for guests. *Represented by:* Bed & Breakfast Hawaii, H-3, (808) 822-1582. $19–$24.

Hawaii. Decorated with curios from around the world and surrounded by 20,000 square feet of tropical plants, this accommodation, which has a private bath, is in the Hilo Hills area. *Represented by:* Bed & Breakfast Hawaii, H-5, (808) 822-1582. $19–$24.

Hawaii. This accommodation in the hills of Kailua consists of a studio apartment with a private bath and entrance. Elevation here is 2,000 feet, which allows one to view the ocean and the sun setting behind it. *Represented by:* Bed & Breakfast Hawaii, H-6, (808) 822-1582. $20–$28.

Hawaii. Convenient to shopping and dining areas, this accommodation is at the edge of a golf course. A pool, Jacuzzi, and tennis courts are available; your host has a car and a moped for rent. *Represented by:* Bed & Breakfast Hawaii, H-7, (808) 822-1582. $20–$25.

Hawaii. A mile or so from Kailua town center, this accommodation on landscaped property is close to tennis courts and a pool. *Represented by:* Bed & Breakfast Hawaii, H-8, (808) 822-1582. $20–$25.

Hawaii. A completely furnished condominium apartment, this accommodation features a 7-by-20-foot veranda that overlooks Snug Harbor. The building has washers and dryers, a pool, a Jacuzzi, and a parking lot. *Represented by:* Bed & Breakfast Hawaii, H-9, (808) 822-1582. $30.50.

Hawaii. Each guest room has a private entrance and a private bath. This year-old home also offers a tennis court, a pool, and a view of the Pacific. *Represented by:* Bed & Breakfast Hawaii, H-10, (808) 822-1582. $30.00–$32.50.

Kauai. This accommodation, minutes from Poipu Beach, features a private entrance and small back patio. The room has a small refrigerator and a color television set. The grounds are marked by well-tended gardens. *Represented by:* Bed & Breakfast Hawaii, K-1, (808) 822-1582. $22–$27.

Kauai. Located behind Sleeping Giant Mountain, this studio apartment is separate from the main house and features a large lanai (veranda). The Wailua River is nearby, as are several parks and hiking trails. *Represented by:* Bed & Breakfast Hawaii, K-3, (808) 822-1582. $20–$30.

Kauai. On a half acre of landscaped property, this accommodation is in a residential area 4 miles from the beach. Two guest rooms are available, and both offer limited use of the kitchen. *Represented by:* Bed & Breakfast Hawaii, K-4, (808) 822-1582. $14–$19.

Kauai. Your host, a marathon runner, is involved in many island activities and looks forward to sharing them with guests. The house is 2 miles from the ocean and the Wailua River, and guests here are offered limited use of the kitchen. *Represented by:* Bed & Breakfast Hawaii, K-5, (808) 822-1582. $15–$20.

Kauai. This one-bedroom condominium on Hanalei Bay with a view of Bali Hai features tennis courts, two pools, and nightly movies. You can rent the studio only or the entire apartment. *Represented by:* Bed & Breakfast Hawaii, K-6, (808) 822-1582. $42–$60.

Kauai. Your hostess, active in community affairs, has a three-bedroom home in the hills above Wailua River. The property, located on a dead-end street, is quite rural. *Represented by:* Bed & Breakfast Hawaii, K-7, (808) 822-1582. $15–$20.

Kauai. Two miles from Poipu Beach, this accommodation features a private entrance, a pullman kitchen, a television set, and a patio. The host, who enjoys hiking, tennis, golf, and swimming, is willing to accompany guests on excursions. *Represented by:* Bed & Breakfast Hawaii, K-8, (808) 822-1582. $20–$27.

Kauai. This accommodation offers a 180-degree view of the mountains and the ocean, as well as a private entrance and a kitchenette. The house is situated in the Lawai hills, on several acres. Your hosts own horses and dogs. *Represented by:* Bed & Breakfast Hawaii, K-10, (808) 822-1582. $42.

Kauai. An old plantation worker's house, this accommodation is on the northern coast of Kauai. A secluded beach is a short walk away. Your hosts, and their dog, are marathon runners. *Represented by:* Bed & Breakfast Hawaii, K-12, (808) 822-1582. $15–$20.

Kauai. This accommodation is a two-bedroom condominum in Princeville. Large windows and glass doors provide lovely views, and the apartment provides linens, cooking utensils, and a washer and dryer. Available for a minimum of four nights, the apartment is in a complex that has tennis courts, a swimming pool, and a golf course. *Represented by:* Bed & Breakfast Hawaii, K-13, (808) 822-1582. $60 (4 nights minimum), $285 weekly.

Kauai. Located in Kilauea, a sleepy town on Kauai's lush northern shore, this accommodation features a private bath, a patio, and full kitchen privileges. *Represented by:* Bed & Breakfast Hawaii, K-15, (808) 822-1582. $20–$25.

Maui. In a residential area across the street from the beach and a short walk from town, this accommodation offers two guest rooms. Guests are allowed limited use of kitchen. *Represented by:* Bed & Breakfast Hawaii, M-1A, (808) 822-1582. $24–$30.

Maui. Two acres of land surround this house, from whose deck you can watch the Pacific Ocean. Minutes from an uncrowded beach, this accommodation offering two rooms will appeal to hikers and countryside explorers. *Represented by:* Bed & Breakfast Hawaii, M-4, (808) 822-1582. $25–$30.

Maui. The grounds of this accommodation are landscaped with fruit trees, berries, vegetables, and local flowers. A patio has a table and chairs, and a sitting room has a television set. *Represented by:* Bed & Breakfast Hawaii, M-7, (808) 822-1582. $24.

Maui. Furnished with mats, pillows, and low tables, this Japanese tea house-style home is three blocks from the ocean. The beds are *futons* (Japanese sleeping quilts), and each guest room has a private outdoor area. Tea ceremony breakfast; outdoor shower. *Represented by:* Bed & Breakfast Hawaii, M-8, (808)

822-1582. $17.50–$20.00.

Maui. A large banyan tree shades the garden of this accommodation, which is a short walk from the beach and also convenient to shops, restaurants, and cafés. Limited use of kitchen. *Represented by:* Bed & Breakfast Hawaii, M-9, (808) 822-1582. $17–$22.

Molokai. This studio cottage, 18 miles east of Kaunakakai, has a refrigerator, cooking facilities, a private bath, and a walk-in closet. On a sandy beach near Halawa Valley this accommodation features a sun porch that overlooks the ocean. Molokai Island. *Represented by:* Bed & Breakfast Hawaii, MO-1, (808) 822-1582. $30–$40.

Oahu. Situated in the Oiea Hills overlooking Pearl Harbor this guest house is 15 minutes from downtown Honolulu and Waikiki. The house features a swimming pool, a garden, and a lanai. Guests are invited to use the pool table and Ping-Pong tables. *Represented by:* Bed & Breakfast Hawaii, O-1 (808) 822-1582. $20–$25.

Oahu. Five minutes from Waikiki in the Honolulu hills, this studio apartment, separate from the main house, features large windows, a kitchen area, and a private patio with a barbecue. *Represented by:* Bed & Breakfast Hawaii, O-2, (808) 822-1582. $25–$30.

Oahu. A three-bedroom home in the hills near Diamond Head, this guest house has a front garden dominated by a large mango tree, as well as a spectacular ocean view. *Represented by:* Bed & Breakfast Hawaii, O-3, (808) 822-1582. $15–$20.

Oahu. With views of Waikiki, Pearl Harbor, and the ocean, this house is high in the hills, 15 minutes from downtown Honolulu (and 10 degrees cooler). *Represented by:* Bed & Breakfast Hawaii, O-4, (808) 822-1582. $22–$27.

Oahu. The entire top floor of this elegantly furnished two-story house is reserved for guests. Each room has television. One has a half bath; and the other, a full bath down the hall. The house features a sitting room, a lanai, and a swimming pool. *Represented by:* Bed & Breakfast Hawaii, O-5, (808) 822-1582. $20–$25.

Oahu. This home, on the west coast of Oahu, has a large backyard that ends at the Pacific Ocean. The yard features a barbecue, as well as a picnic table and benches. The guest room has an indoor ceramic-tiled lanai, a refrigerator, color television, and a private bath. *Represented by:* Bed & Breakfast Hawaii, O-6 (808) 822-1582. $25–$30.

Oahu. This is an apartment separate from the main house. The grounds feature a garden and a swimming pool, and the apartment has its own cooking facilities, as well as a private entrance. The beach is within walking distance. *Represented by:* Bed & Breakfast Hawaii, O-7, (808) 822-1582. $22.50–$27.50.

Oahu. Within walking distance of the beach, this home is surrounded by a large garden sprinkled with fruit trees. A bus that stops nearby can take you quickly into Honolulu. *Represented by:* Bed & Breakfast Hawaii, O-8, (808) 822-1582. $18–$22.

Oahu. A short walk from this home will get you to a large shopping mall, and an even shorter walk, a few steps in fact, will bring you to a small private beach. The house has a large lanai. *Represented by:* Bed & Breakfast Hawaii, O-9, (808) 822-1582. $25–$40.

Oahu. The main house, which has two guest rooms, is an A-frame structure perched on a cliff immediately overlooking the ocean. The hosts also have a studio cottage available for guests. *Represented by:* Bed & Breakfast Hawaii, O-12, (808) 822-1582. Main house $22–$27, cottage $40.

Kauai (#10) (*Bed & Breakfast Hawaii*)

The Greyhouse Inn

Star Route, Box 16, Salmon, ID 83467. (208) 756-3968.
Hosts: Robert and Vera Slicton.

Idaho's Salmon River Country is a maze of hills and valleys. Its verdant springs and summers attract trout and steelhead fishers, and its snowy winters draw cross country and downhill skiers. Float excursions on the Middle Fork and Salmon rivers are perhaps the areas most popular attraction.

In 1894, a German brewery and ice-house entrepreneur built The Greyhouse Inn—an eleven-room farmhouse with a gabled, multiangular roof. The house used to be located in the town of Salmon, where it served over the years as a beauty shop, a boardinghouse, and even for a time as the town hospital. Relocated in 1970 to 12 miles outside of town, the house has been restored to its turn-of-the-century condition.

Authentic late-nineteenth-century and early-twentieth-century frontier furniture appears throughout the inn, as do elegant wallcoverings and thick-piled floral design carpeting. One guest room has a sitting room and a balcony; the other has an old parlor stove. Both have beautiful mountain views.

The Slictons take pleasure in arranging trips and activities for their guests, with whom they enjoy sharing wine in their sitting room. They also operate a small antique and crafts shop.

Accommodations: 2 rooms with shared bath. *Smoking:* Not permitted. *Children:* Not permitted. *Pets:* Not permitted. *Breakfast:* Included. *Driving Instructions:* From Salmon, take Route 28 east; turn south on Route 93 and go 12 miles to milepost 293.

Lakefront. This architecturally interesting apartment, with molded plaster walls and ceilings, overlooks Chicago's lakefront and Belmont Harbor. The guest room features a four-poster bed and a private bath, and the apartment's location is convenient; it's only 5 minutes away from the Loop. The hostess, a businesswoman, enjoys cooking and decorating. *Represented by:* Bed & Breakfast Chicago, (312) 328-1321 or 446-9139. $40.

Lincoln Park. An 1890s building transformed into four separate apartments, this guest house offers three apartments for guests—one with one bedroom and two with two bedrooms. The two-bedroom apartments have living rooms and dining areas, and the one-bedroom apartment has a wet bar instead of a kitchen. The building is on Holsted Street, close to Fullerton. *Represented by:* Bed & Breakfast Chicago, (312) 328-1321 or 446-9139. $50.

Evanston. The hosts, who buy and sell estates, have a Tudor-style home that faces a forest preserve. They offer guests a suite with two bedrooms—one of which has wood paneling and an exposed-beam ceiling—and a single bedroom, with a private bath, that overlooks their yard and patio. The Loop is only 20 minutes away. *Represented by:* Bed & Breakfast Chicago, (312) 328-1321 or 446-9139. $30–$45.

Evanston. Built in 1892, this row house is owned by a professional caterer who will prepare dinners for guests who so request. Two bedrooms, done in Colonial motifs, are available for guests, and the sitting room has a fireplace. Public transportation is nearby. *Represented by:* Bed & Breakfast Chicago, (312) 328-1321 or 446-9139. $30–$45.

Evanston. Two blocks from Lake Michigan and five from Northwestern University, this accommodation is in an 1890s townhouse in Evanston's historic district. The hosts are a professional couple who have traveled a great deal. *Represented by:* Bed & Breakfast Chicago, (312) 328-1321 or 446-9139. $30–$45.

Glencoe. At once rural and convenient, this Cape Cod-style house is owned by an artist, whose watercolor landscapes hang here and there. The guest room features a sitting area, television, and a four-poster covered with a handmade quilt. A breakfast room overlooks a garden with bird feeders, but when the weather's right, the morning meal is served in the sun parlor.

Evanston Historic District (*Bed & Breakfast Chicago*)

Glencoe Cape Cod (*Bed & Breakfast Chicago*)

Represented by: Bed & Breakfast Chicago, (312) 328-1321 or 446-9139. $35–$50.

Glencoe. This Colonial-style home has a private beach and a host whose hobbies—quilting and needlework—contribute substantially to the home's decor. The guest room, which has a fireplace, overlooks Lake Michigan. *Represented by:* Bed & Breakfast Chicago, (312) 328-1321 or 446-9139. $35–$50.

Wilmette. The host, an artist, invites guests to peruse his sculpture studio, which is adjacent to his house. The house features a large kitchen filled with antiques. There is also a greenhouse with a fireplace. The house is convenient to public transportation, which can get you into central Chicago in 30 minutes. *Represented by:* Bed & Breakfast Chicago, (312) 328-1321 or 446-9139. $35.

Winnetka. This custom-designed house, which was built using a great deal of glass, is obviously owned by somebody with a green thumb: A profusion of flora surrounds the house and the driveway. The host offers three guest rooms with air conditioning and television. *Represented by:* Bed & Breakfast Chicago, (312) 328-1321 or 446-9139. $30–$50.

Winnetka. Convenient to the Chicago Botanic Garden, this accommodation is hosted by a part-time librarian. The decor is traditional. A short walk brings you to public transportation, which can get you into Chicago in less than an hour. *Represented by:* Bed & Breakfast Chicago, (312) 328-1321 or 446-9139. $25–$30.

Wilmette (*Bed & Breakfast Chicago*)

Hobson's Bluffdale

Eldred, IL 62027. (217) 983-2854. *Hosts:* Bill and Lindy Hobson.

Hobson's Bluffdale is a 320-acre, working farm. The farmhouse, an 1828 stone structure, was built by Bill Hobson's great-great-great-grandfather, an American officer who fought in the War of 1812. The house has six fireplaces made of local limestone. Very local limestone: you can see the limestone bluffs, on the other side of the river, from the Hobsons' front yard.

The backyard has a heated swimming pool, a whirlpool bath, a basketball court, a bonfire area, and, for swingers, rope-swings hanging from large trees. The backyard blends into thick woods where hikers or joggers or horseback riders find miles of scenic trails.

The Hobsons enjoy organized activities like bonfires or hayrides or picnics: It's not uncommon for them to prepare a box lunch for everybody and take guests motorboating or canoeing down the Illinois River.

Rates here, based on weekly occupancy, include all meals. Once a week the Hobsons roast a hog.

Accommodations: 3 suites and 5 family-size rooms, all with private bath. *Smoking:* Permitted except in the main house. *Children:* Permitted. *Pets:* Not permitted. *Breakfast:* Included. *Driving Instructions:* From Carrouton proceed west; at Eldred go north for 3 1/2 miles.

Galena **ILLINOIS**

Colonial Guest House and Antique Shop

1004 Park Avenue, Galena, IL 61036. (815) 777-0336. *Hostess:* Mary Keller.

The Colonial Guest House, a large 1826 Greek Revival structure, has two 36-foot screened-in porches and columns in front. It is fronted by two large pine trees and gaslights imported from

England. Its Victorian antique furnishings include a great deal of art and pattern glass and china and silver. Mary Keller has been in the antique business all her life and operates a shop on the premises. Her home, photographed by *P.M.* magazine, appeared on national television. Oriental rugs, Victorian furniture upholstered in velvet, and chandeliers and similar appointments characterize the kind of furnishings one would expect to find in an antique dealer's home. Mary doesn't serve breakfast, but coffee is always available. Each guest room has a private entrance.

Mary's front windows have a panoramic view of the city of Galena, which has several museums as well as theaters and antique shops. General Ulysses S. Grant's home is nearby, as are the Chestnut Mountain Ski resort and several public golf courses.

Accommodations: 4 rooms with private bath. *Smoking:* Permitted. *Children:* Permitted. *Pets:* Permitted only if small. *Driving Instructions:* On Route 20, at the Eastend Bridge.

Cooling Residence

1008 Ina Avenue, Princeton, IL 61356. (815) 875-1879.

Hosts: Mr. and Mrs. Robert Cooling.

The Cooling Residence is a ten-room split-level contemporary house surrounded by a manicured lawn and hedges. The front lawn features a young red maple tree and a flower bed with red petunias and salvias.

Robert Cooling is a Lutheran minister, and his wife, Sylvia, teaches piano. Sundays, Mrs. Cooling plays the organ at her husband's church, Saint Matthew's. She prefers playing piano music by Mozart and Hayden, and Bach and Handel wrote her favorite organ pieces. The Coolings' piano is in their casually furnished family room. The parlor, fully carpeted in brown and gold, has a color television set, an extra-large sofa, a recliner, and a swivel rocker. Its walls are covered with a combination of wood paneling and flocked gold wallpaper. The entire house is air-conditioned, and the Coolings serve guests a Continental breakfast. As Mrs. Cooling puts it, The "children have grown, married, and left this rambling house to Mom, Dad and two dachshunds."

Accommodations: 4 rooms, 2 with private bath. *Smoking:* Not permitted. *Children:* Permitted. *Pets:* Permitted if small and well behaved. *Breakfast:* Included. *Driving Instructions:* Take Route I-80 to Princeton.

Bill and Jean Akers

653 South Main Street, Crown Point, IN 46307. (219) 663-3999. *Hosts:* Bill and Jean Akers.

The Akerses have a 1929 Cape Cod–style house, with a long sloping gable that ends at a bay window. The house is on an archetypal midwestern Main Street, complete with elms, maples, and wide thoroughfares.

Bill is a recently retired elementary school principal, and Jean is personnel director of the Lake Company government complex. They decided to open their home to guests after vacationing in Canada, where they stayed at several impressive bed-and-breakfast places.

Bill describes his furnishings as modern eclectic. One guest room and the dining room are decorated in pecan wood French Provincial. The entire house is carpeted wall-to-wall and centrally air-conditioned. The central parlor, which has a couch, a love seat, and several overstuffed armchairs, features a Hammond organ, which Jean plays—sometimes. Bill's hobbies are making fine jewelry and gourmet cooking. The Akerses serve a complimentary breakfast, and their home is near several local historical attractions and an hour's drive from Chicago.

Accommodations: 2 rooms, 1 with private bath. *Smoking:* Permitted. *Children:* Permitted. *Pets:* Not permitted. *Breakfast:* Included. *Driving Instructions:* The house is 1¼ miles south of the Old Court House on Main Street.

Camel Lot

4512 West 131st Street, Westfield, IN 46074. (317) 873-4370. *Host:* Moselle Schaeffer.

You won't run into Launcelot or Guinevere or Merlin as you wander about the 50-acre grounds of Camel Lot, but you will very likely bump into Jane Doe, a resident deer. A working animal-breeding farm, Camel Lot has (in addition to what the pun implies) llamas, zebras, and other exotic quadrupeds.

Moselle has one guest accommodation—a three-room suite with a bedroom, a television room, and a private bath. The bedroom is furnished with antiques including a grand old four-poster bed. A complimentary breakfast includes freshly squeezed orange juice, coffee, and homemade bread. When the weather is good, Moselle serves breakfast on the terrace, which overlooks Ivan's cage. Ivan is a Siberian tiger. What's Moselle like? You have to Noah to love her. A guest who stayed at Camel Lot put it this way: "It worked out great—she's into breeding tigers, and I'm into breeding fresh air."

Accommodations: 1 suite with private bath. *Smoking:* Permitted. *Children:* Over 10 permitted. *Pets:* Permitted by prior arrangement. *Driving Instructions:* Take Meridian Street to 131st Street (proceeding north); turn west on 131st Street and go 4½ miles.

Hotel Brooklyn

154 Front Street, Brooklyn, IA 52211. (515) 522-9229. *Hostess:* Kathryn Lawson.

The Hotel Brooklyn is an 1875 brick Victorian structure with buttressed gables, a three-story tower, and four Doric columns supporting its porch and pediment. The building, in the National register of Historic Places, was originally erected as a home but later served as a hospital. The sitting room has a marble fireplace, mahogany and walnut furniture, and handpainted murals. Fine woodwork is found throughout the house, which features a grand old central staircase.

Two of the nine guest rooms have private baths; all have television sets and air conditioning. Each guest room features at least one genuine antique—a 100-year-old dresser here, a 125-year-old easy chair there.

Kathy has been in the hotel business since 1940 and told me that this year her establishment has entertained guests from twenty-two different countries. Can city-dodgers find something to do in Brooklyn? Yes, provided they enjoy lakes, swimming pools, golf courses, and parks. The Hotel Brooklyn is a half hour from the Amana colonies, a group of seven small villages formed by mid-nineteenth-century German emigrés who came to this country to escape persecution.

Accommodations: 9 rooms, 2 with private bath. *Smoking:* Permitted. *Children:* Permitted. *Pets:* Not permitted. *Driving Instructions:* Two miles from Route I-80, or a mile from Route 6.

Bed and Breakfast on Our Farm

Route 1, Wakefield, Kansas 67487. (913) 461-5596. *Hosts:* Rod and Pearl Thurlow.

"We're not a guesting ranch," says Pearl Thrulow, "but just a plain farm family who really like people, and especially children." Rod and Pearl live in a hundred-year-old midwestern farmhouse, situated on 160 acres of land. The Thrulows raise wheat, soybeans, oats, pigs, cattle, and chickens. They grow just about all of their own food, grind their own wheat flour for baking, and use raw milk. Pearl assured me that cookies, homemade ice cream, baked goods, and juice, milk, and coffee are there anytime guests want them. Rod and Pearl serve a hearty breakfast each morning; and for late sleepers they leave about the kitchen all the makings of a morning meal.

Pearl and Rod's daughter and husband own a nearby ninety-cow dairy farm, which Pearl enjoys sharing with her guests. The Thurlows don't follow a set schedule: "We do what is most important for that day—it may be haying or it may be a family picnic."

Pearl's and Rod's farm is close to the Eisenhower home, the Tuttle Creek and Milford dams' water facilities, Fort Riley, and one of the country's most important archeological sites—a prehistoric Indian burial pit near Salina.

Accommodations: 3 rooms with shared bath. *Smoking:* Permitted. *Children:* Permitted. *Pets:* Permitted. *Breakfast:* Included. *Driving Instructions:* From Junction City, take Route I-70; take exit 286; proceed 9 miles to the county line; then go 1 mile east and 1/3 mile north, to the first farm on the west side of the road.

Asphodel Village

Route 2, Box 89. Jackson, LA 70748. (504) 654-6868. *Host:* Mack Couhig.

William Carlos Williams began what sensible critics consider his best poem with these lines: "Of Asphodel, that greeny flower, I have come to speak." The asphodel, according to Greek mythology, was the flower of heaven, the Greeks' Elysian fields.

Asphodel Village consists of five buildings. The main antebellum plantation house, which took ten years to build, was completed around 1830. When the Couhigs took over the property, they moved to it from the nearby town of Jackson a structure called the Levy House, built in 1780. In order to be moved, it had to be cut into three pieces and then reassembled.

Asphodel Village has 500 acres of grounds, with trails winding among hills and creeks. The property also has three guest houses, designed by Mrs. Couhig, who incorporated into the structures antique doors and windows that she acquired in New Orleans. All the guest rooms, some of which are cottages surrounded by pine trees and flowering dogwood, have private baths and individually controlled air conditioning and heat.

The Couhigs serve a complimentary full country breakfast to guests. Their facilities include a gift shop and a restaurant where, for a price, items like beef balls Burgundy or crabmeat crepes are available.

Accommodations: 10 rooms with private bath. *Smoking:* Permitted. *Children:* Permitted. *Pets:* Not permitted. *Breakfast:* Included. *Driving Instructions:* From Baton Rouge, proceed north on Route 61; turn right onto Route 68 and follow it for 8 miles.

New Orleans **LOUISIANA**

Cornstalk Fence Guest House

915 Royal Street, New Orleans, LA 70116. (504) 523-1515. *Hostess:* Mrs. Rosina Noble.

Once upon a time, about 150 years ago, as a matter of fact, a wealthy man from Iowa built a cast-iron fence for his new bride. He brought her from Iowa to live with him in New Orleans, and he wanted her to see, through the windows of her new home, cornstalks entwined with morning glories, which is what she had grown up seeing. Everybody knows there ain't no cornstalks in New Orleans, so the wealthy man from Iowa had incredible facsimiles thereof cast in iron. The fence must be seen to be believed. You can almost hear it growing. Many years later, a writer stayed in this house, and while she was there she wrote a novel—*Uncle Tom's Cabin.*

The house is a *circa* 1780 Georgian, with four large Ionic columns holding up the second-floor balcony, where you may have your complimentary breakfast if you like. All rooms have high ceilings, fireplaces, and antique furnishings.

In the heart of New Orleans's French Quarter, the Cornstalk Fence Guest House is right next door to some of America's best food and jazz.

Accommodations: 14 rooms with private bath. *Smoking:* Permitted. *Children:* Permitted. *Pets:* Not permitted. *Breakfast:* Included. *Driving Instructions:* Take Route I-10 to the French Quarter; proceed to Royal Street.

New Orleans **LOUISIANA**

Lafitte Guest House

1003 Bourbon Street, New Orleans, LA 70116. (504) 581-2678. *Host:* Steve Guyton.

Built in the grand old tradition of brick French Quarter houses, the Lafitte Guest House was completed by master builder Joshua Peebles in 1849. The house, on the corner of Bourbon and Saint Phillip streets, has wrought ironwork on its balconies, 14-foot ceilings, black marble and carved-mahogany mantels, crystal chandeliers, and many antiques.

Some guest rooms feature entrances to the landscaped courtyard, windows overlooking it, or, in some cases, private entrances. All guest rooms are carpeted, air-conditioned (a must in New Orleans), and have telephones. The Guytons offer a complimentary breakfast (freshly squeezed orange juice, French roast coffee, a croissant or a brioche), which is served to you in your room. The Lafitte Guest House also has parking facilities (as badly needed as air conditioning in New Orleans's French Quarter).

As lovely as this guest house is, its location is even lovelier—it is within walking distance of but not intruded upon by the frenetic activity of Bourbon Street. Food and jazz are always close at hand, as is the staff.

Accommodations: 14 rooms with private bath. *Smoking:* Permitted. *Children:* Permitted. *Pets:* Not permitted. *Breakfast:* Included. *Driving Instructions:* Take Route 1-10 to the French Quarter; proceed to the intersection of Bourbon and Saint Phillip streets.

New Orleans **LOUISIANA**

Park View Guest House

7004 St. Charles Avenue, New Orleans, LA 70118. (504) 866-5580. *Host:* J. Phillips IV.

A large, rambling Victorian structure with steep gables and column-supported balconies on two floors, the Park View Guest House was built in 1892. Inspired, rumor has it, by the 1884 World's Fair, held across the street in Audubon Park, the building first functioned as Widow Corey Taylor's Boarding Home. The house today is replete with Victoriana, such as mahogany woodwork, crystal chandeliers, stained glass, beveled glass, and fireplaces. Guest rooms are furnished with a combination of period reproductions and genuine antiques. Several rooms have fireplaces, some have private or shared balconies, and some feature large, low-silled windows overlooking Audubon Park.

The Park View Guest House is on historic Saint Charles Avenue, immediately across the street from Tulane and Loyola universities and Dominican College. The oldest surviving streetcar system in the country runs along Saint Charles Avenue, and in twenty minutes it will take you from the Park View's front door to the French Quarter.

Each morning, in the central dining room, the hosts serve a complimentary Continental breakfast.

Accommodations: 25 rooms, 14 with private bath. *Smoking:* Permitted. *Children:* Permitted. *Pets:* Not permitted. *Breakfast:* Included. *Driving Instructions:* Take Saint Charles Avenue uptown toward the Univer-Section, to the corner of Audubon Park and Saint Charles.

623 Ursulines

623 Ursulines Street, New Orleans, LA 70116. (504) 529-5489. *Hosts:* Jim Weirich and Don Heil.

Having purchased the property from Ursuline nuns, Joseph Guillot, a New Orleans contractor, built this 1825 French Quarter town house. The facade features iron railings and gateways. Flagstone-paved alleyways lead from the street to the large private courtyard, which each guest suite opens onto. It is lushly planted with magnolias and orchids, and azaleas, palms, and other subtropical plants. All manner of birds congregate around the courtyard's feeders and birdbath. Each guest suite has a bedroom, a sitting area, a private bath, and a kitchenette and is air-conditioned.

Jim and Don do not include breakfast in their rates, but they do offer a morning paper. Like any interesting city, New Orleans can be baffling to visitors, so they make a point of directing their guests to the many places most worth visiting in this town.

Accommodations; 7 rooms with private bath. *Smoking:* Permitted. *Children:* Over 12 permitted. *Pets:* Permitted if well-behaved. *Driving Instructions:* Take Route I-10 to the French Quarter and proceed to Ursulines Street.

The Brannon-Bunker Inn

Box 045, Route 129, Damariscotta, ME 04543. (207) 563-5941. *Hosts:* Dave and Char Bunker.

The Brannon-Bunker Inn, which is open May through October, consists of an 1820 Cape-style house, an attached barn, and a small carriage house on the other side of an old footbridge. During the 1920s the barn was a dance hall called La Hacienda.

Furnished for the most part with period antiques, the house contains such features as pineapple-post beds, an Empire chest and mirror, a corner cabinet filled with antique Strawberry dishes and pewter, a sleigh bed, reproduction period wallpapers, and an old ice chest that's been converted into a bar. Dave and Char don't serve liquor, but they provide guests with all the set-ups they need, and sometimes they bring out hors d'oeuvres.

The living room, whose furnishings change from year to year, is dominated by a fieldstone fireplace around which guests tend to congregate.

Several of the guest rooms—particularly the two new rooms in the old carriage house—have views of the Damariscotta River. One of these new rooms features a pineapple-post bed, and the other comes complete with a kitchen area.

Accommodations: 6 rooms, 3 with private bath. *Smoking:* Permitted. *Children:* Permitted. *Pets:* Permitted if well behaved. *Breakfast:* Included. *Driving Instructions:* Follow Business Route 1 through the town of Damariscotta, then take Route 129 south.

Kennebunkport **MAINE**

The Chetwynd House

Chestnut Street, Box 130, Kennebunkport, ME 04046. (207) 967-2235. *Hostess:* Susan Knowles Chetwynd.

The Chetwynd House is an 1840 Colonial structure originally built by Captain Matthew Seavey. Abbott Graves, the artist, owned it in the early twentieth century. The house features a handsome staircase, floor-to-ceiling windows, and pumpkin-pine floors. The rooms are furnished in country Colonial, with predominately mahogany and cherry pieces. Susan Chetwynd characterizes the color scheme as consisting of "lots of blues and white, with touches of red, gold, and celery."

A former high school English teacher who moved to Maine from Connecticut, Susan has a large collection of books, and she keeps the oral tradition alive at her breakfast table. She claims many of her guests get so full at breakfast that they have no choice but to skip their lunch. Hot chocolate and tea are available when it's cold, and Susan serves wine and cheese in her garden when it's warm.

Accommodations: 4 rooms, 1 with private bath. *Smoking:* Permitted. *Children:* Not permitted. *Pets:* Not permitted. *Breakfast:* Included. *Driving Instructions:* From Kennebunkport's Dock Square, follow the signs for Ocean Avenue—Chestnut Street is the second street off it.

The 1802 House

Box 774, Locke Street, Kennebunkport, ME 04046. (207) 967-5632. *Hosts:* Robert and Charlotte Houle.

The 1802 House, a large structure whose top half is painted marine blue and whose bottom half is covered with natural cedar shingles, used to be 20 miles from where it now stands. A team of oxen dragged the house all the way from Waterboro to Kennebunkport, and they must have pulled the house gently because its original walnut staircase is still intact.

The house is furnished with reproduction Colonial pieces, and each guest room has reproduction wallpaper color-coordinated with the bedspreads, linens, and curtains. All these rooms are carpeted wall to wall, and each has a private bath. One guest room has a fireplace with an antique oval mirror hanging above it and a large sitting pillow immediately in front of it, two maple double beds, reproduction Colonial ship-print wallpaper, and a view of the river. Each of the guest rooms has at least one green plant in it, and there's a profusion of plants in front of the glass doors in the dining-and-sitting area, which has a rust and brown carpet that matches the colors of the couch's upholstery. At a large table in this room a full country breakfast is served every morning.

The 1802 House has a lawn with umbrellaed tables and plenty of room to relax. Guests would do well to forsake their cars and either bicycle or walk around the area, which offers many attractions, including an eighteen-hole golf course right next door to the 1802 House.

Accommodations: 8 rooms with private bath. *Smoking:* Permitted except in the breakfast room. *Children:* Under twelve not permitted. *Pets:* Not permitted. *Breakfast:* Included. *Driving Instructions:* Take exit 3 off the Maine Turnpike, then Route 35 into Kennebunkport; turn left at the Sunoco station, then left on North Street, and look for the red-and-white sign just after passing the church.

Olde Rowley Inn

Route 135, Junction of Route 118, North Waterford, ME 04267. (207) 583-4143. *Hosts:* Michael and Debra Lennon.

Built in 1790 by stagecoach driver John Rice, the Olde Rowley Inn is a clapboard building that used to service the White Mountains stagecoach line. The living room has a large brick fireplace, a beehive oven, wide-board pine floors, and a mixture of genuine antiques and period reproductions. The room has an overstuffed reproduction Colonial sofa, antique oaken tables and rockers, and a bookcase dating back to the mid-nineteenth century.

A tightwinder staircase leads up to the guest rooms, which have exposed-beam ceilings and pumpkin pine floors and are lighted by electrified tin lanterns. The guest rooms feature reproduction wallpapers and, like the living room, are furnished with a combination of period reproductions and genuine antiques, such as a four-poster and oaken dressers from the early nineteenth century. One room has a four-poster, antique Windsor chairs, crocheted pillows, and white Cape Cod curtains that soften the morning sun.

The inn also has a bar constructed of wood from a barn, as well as a dining room with a wood-burning stove.

Accommodations: 5 rooms with shared bath. *Smoking:* Permitted. *Children:* Check in advance. *Pets:* Not permitted. *Breakfast:* Included. *Driving Instructions:* The Olde Rowley Inn is in North Waterford a hundred yards or so from the junction of Routes 135 and 118.

Blue Shutters

6 Beachmere Place, Box 655, Ogunquit, ME 03907. (207) 646-2163. *Hosts:* Ronald and Jean Dahler

Blue Shutters, a large and typically New England–style structure, is on a quiet residential street at the edge of Ogunquit. A path in the backyard connects with the Marginal Way, a blacktopped pathway, with shrubbery and wild roses beside it, that follows the Maine coast, which is spectacular hereabouts. Blue Shutters's guests are invited to use the private beaches, one of them three minutes from the house, off the Marginal Way.

After passing through an Oriental-style entrance, dominated by a large blue-and-white Oriental rug, guests enter the living room. Done in shades of blue, that room has a flowered couch and a couple of overstuffed easy chairs facing a fireplace.

The guest rooms all have ocean views. Two guest rooms have fireplaces, and one has French doors that open onto a private deck. The rooms feature some Colonial furniture, oil paintings and prints hang here and there, and each room is color-coordinated. Ronald and Jean also offer six efficiency cottages with fully equipped cooking facilities. Breakfast, served on English china, is brought to your room at whatever time you feel like being awakened.

Accommodations: 5 rooms with private bath, 6 cottages. *Smoking:* Permitted. *Children:* Sometimes permitted (check in advance). *Pets:* Not permitted. *Breakfast:* Included. *Driving Instructions:* Take Route 1 into Ogunquit Village Square, turn at the light, and proceed toward Perkins Cove. Go 0.4 mile, and Beachmere Place will be on your left.

High Tor

Frazier Pasture Road, Ogunquit, ME 03907. (207) 646-8232. *Hostesses:* Julie O'Brien and Cleda Farris Wiley.

A 1913 Cape Cod–style structure with a column-supported overhang forming a veranda, High Tor is constructed entirely of natural wood. The building, on an acre of pines and wild bushes and berries, overlooks a mile-long coastal footpath known as the Marginal Way. The property's 190-foot artesian well draws 100 percent–tested pure springwater.

The central living room, which is 30 feet long, features a fieldstone fireplace and exposed ceiling-beams. Of an afternoon, Julie and Cleda often start a fire and serve complimentary wine to their guests. All guest rooms have ocean views, private baths, and individually controlled heating. They all have comfortable beds and are furnished with New England country antiques.

High Tor's location is at once convenient and secluded—the towns of Ogunquit and Perkins Cove are short walks away, and a 500-foot-long path leads from the property to the ocean. Julie and Cleda serve guests a complimentary breakfast.

Accommodations: 3 rooms with private bath. *Smoking:* Permitted. *Children:* Not permitted. *Pets:* Not permitted. *Breakfast:* Included. *Driving Instructions:* Proceed south from Ogunquit a half mile to Stearns Road; turn left, then take first right onto Cherry Lane; take first left on Frazier Pasture Road; watch for the sign on a pine tree.

Breezemere Farm

South Brooksville, ME 04617. (207) 326-8828. *Hosts:* Jim and Joan Lipke.

Breezemere Farm consists of an 1850 farmhouse with an attached shed and barn. The 60-acre property, in the beautiful Penobscot Bay area, also has six guest cottages, each with a private bath and a Franklin stove or a fireplace. On the grounds are a pine forest, an apple orchard, and a meadow that runs down to the sea. If you don't feel like playing badminton or croquet or horseshoes, the Lipkes will gladly let you take out a rowboat or a sailboat or a bicycle. It's amazing at how many smog-bound urbanites have never seen the Milky Way or a sky exploding with stars, Joan notes.

The farmhouse is furnished with genuine early American antiques. A fieldstone fireplace in the lodge burns 3-foot logs. The complimentary breakfast includes Breezemere granola and blueberry pancakes with real maple syrup. A nearby charter boat will take you to where seals play, or you can explore Arcadia National Park.

Accommodations: 13 rooms, 6 with private bath. *Smoking:* Permitted. *Children:* Permitted. *Pets:* Permitted in cottages only. *Breakfast:* Included. *Driving Instructions:* Take Route 176 from North Brooksville to South Brooksville.

Chevy Chase, Maryland. This spacious modernistic home whose hosts speak French and Hebrew, as well as English, is made of orange crates and has an indoor pool and a sun deck that overlooks the surrounding woods. *Represented by:* Sweet Dreams & Toast, (202) 363-4712. $40.

Annapolis, Maryland. Furnished with Victorian antiques and reproductions, this house is in the heart of Annapolis. All of that city's attractions are within walking distance, as is public transportation. *Represented by:* Sweet Dreams & Toast, (202) 363-4712. $35–40.

Annapolis, Maryland. This 1838 mini-mansion is on 7 acres of land. The hosts have two cats, two German shepherds and six peacocks. *Represented by:* Sweet Dreams & Toast, (202) 363-4712. $25–$50.

New Market **MARYLAND**

Strawberry Inn

17 Main Street, Box 237, New Market, MD 21774. (301) 865-3318. *Hosts:* Ed and Jane Rossig.

An electrical engineer who tired of serving in corporate management, Ed Rossig decided to open an inn. He and his wife, Jane, restored this mid-nineteenth-century Victorian home. Ed and Jane have a picture-framing business and an interest in an antique business. There are some forty-six antique stores in the small town of New Market, and the Strawberry Inn looks like one of them.

The building is furnished with antiques and period reproductions. Brass beds, wide-plank floors, reproduction wallpapers, hand-stenciled baseboards and ceiling moldings, bay windows—touches like these appear throughout the inn. Another nice touch is the Rossigs' complimentary breakfast, which you may have in the dining room or served to you in bed. The Rossigs, at an hour you specify, place a breakfast tray at your door.

Accommodations: 5 rooms with private bath. *Smoking:* Permitted. *Children:* Over 5 permitted. *Pets:* Not permitted. *Breakfast:* Included. *Driving Instructions:* From Frederick, take Route 1-70 east for 7 miles; take exit 60 and follow the signs to New Market.

Near Boston College. Myra, who teaches art and paints, and James, who works in a high-technology industry, invite guests into their split-level contemporary home on a tree-lined dead-end street. They offer a large bedroom with a queen-size bed and a private bath. Their home is furnished with modern pieces, and there is a marked exotic feeling about the place. Although there's no telling what their Siamese cat enjoys, Myra and James are fond of music and art, as well as gourmet cooking, of which guests, for far less than what an average restaurant charges, can take advantage. *Represented by:* New England Bed & Breakfast, (617) 244-2112. $22.00–$42.50.

15 Minutes from Downtown. The nearest subway station is a 1-minute walk from Margaret's house in Newton Centre, and you can get to downtown Boston in 15 minutes. Born in Nova Scotia, Margaret used to run a delicatessen in Newton, and of late she's been spending the better part of her free time doing work for the Catholic Church. Margaret bakes her own muffins and offers guests a room with twin beds. *Represented by:* New England Bed & Breakfast, (617) 244-2112. $21.50–$42.00.

Stone House. Mildred is a retired schoolteacher who lives in a stone house 5 minutes from the subway. Her living room has a fireplace and a stereo Mildred acquired because she loves classical music. The house is filled with artifacts and objets d'art from all over the world. Mildred's interests include mountain climbing, backpacking, and scuba diving. Another hobby is sharing wine with guests while Mozart's music plays in the background. *Represented by:* New England Bed & Breakfast, (617) 244-2112. $21–$41.

Margaret's Room. John and Margo own and operate the New England Bed and Breakfast guest-house agency. John is also executive director of a private social-service agency, and Margo is a travel-promotion specialist. The room they offer guests used to be the quarters of their maid Margaret and has a private bath and a private entrance. A gourmet cook, John tells me his favorite pastime is sitting on the porch while drinking wine and talking about food and travel. I've never tasted his cooking, but I've always enjoyed John's conversation. *Represented by:* New England Bed & Breakfast, (617) 244-2112. $22–$41.

15 Minutes from Downtown (*New England Bed & Breakfast*)

Near Boston College (*New England Bed & Breakfast*)

Arlington (*New England Bed & Breakfast*)

Margaret's Room (*New England Bed & Breakfast*)

Boston Balcony. Almost entirely obscured by evergreens, Jennie's house is a short drive from downtown Boston and within easy walking distance of the subway. She has a thick Austrian accent, and her taste in silver and crystal seems to reflect the Old World heritage her voice evokes. Jennie offers guests a suite of rooms with a balcony, where many of them like to eat breakfast. The living room is quite large, with big vases filled with dried flowers here and there and many mirrors. *Represented by:* New England Bed & Breakfast, (617) 244-2112. $24–$43.

Cambridge. Close to Harvard Square (one of the country's more interesting intersections), this guest house is hosted by a nurse and a caterer. Don recently started a catering business called Seasoned to Taste, and his culinary ambitions show immediately in his kitchen, which is nothing less than encyclopedic in its collection of utensils. As is true of many of Cambridge's houses, the outside of Don and Gina's looks grim, but the inside certainly does not. *Represented by:* New England Bed & Breakfast, (617) 244-2112. $21–$39.

Cambridge. A short walk from Harvard Square, this guest house offers a room with a private bath. The host and hostess are Jane, who has a career as a nurse, and Bob, who is a school psychologist in the Cambridge school system. They have four children, two of whom are usually away at college. Their home features an open back porch where they serve breakfast when the weather's nice. *Represented by:* New England Bed & Breakfast, (617) 244-2112. $21–$39.

Arlington. Joe and Ingebord are in the process of restoring their home, which has floors and walls and even a staircase made of wood. They've done such things as exposing the brick wall in the kitchen and refinishing the staircase. The house features a back porch where, weather permitting, breakfast is served. *Represented by:* New England B & B (617) 244-2112. $21–$39.

Arlington. This two-family home, 10 minutes from Harvard Square by bus, is on a quiet residential street. Naomi is in the health-food field, and Elain is a psychiatric social worker. Both women enjoy music and cooking, and they share a penchant for observing the flutter of activity around the bird feeder on their front porch. Naomi and Elain's guest room has a private bath. *Represented by:* New England B & B (617) 244-2112. $22–$40.

Brewster. The hostess here enjoys helping guests plan their Cape Cod sightseeing, and her house is an ideal base for Cape explorers. The National Seashore beaches are half an hour away; but the local beach is within less than a mile, and the town of Brewster offers guests plenty of good restaurants and other attractions. The guest room has a private bath. *Represented by:* Houseguests Cape Cod, Host Home #2, (617) 385-8332. $25–$35.

Dennis. This accommodation on Cape Cod's historic highway includes a bedroom, living room, kitchen, private bath, and private patio. The Victorian house has landscaped grounds. *Represented by:* Houseguests Cape Cod, House Guest Home #1, (617) 385-8332. $50.

Dennis. A new but antique-filled home decorated by a professional, this house is only minutes from the Dennis beaches. The guest suite contains a private bath, a living room with television, a kitchen, and a private entrance. The house has a deck, filled with flowers and always available for use by guests. *Represented by:* Houseguests Cape Cod, Host Guest Quarters #1, (617) 385-8332. Weekly only—$225–$250.

Dennis Port. This guest house features a private beach on Nantucket Sound, a picnic table and barbecue, and a Florida-type room for relaxing at day's end. In addition to the swimming, facilities for golf, biking, and fishing are nearby. The hostess is fluent in French and German, as well as English. *Represented by:* Houseguests Cape Cod, Host Home #2, (617) 385-8332. Weekly only, $200.

Dennis Port. Within walking distance of the south-side beaches, as well as restaurants, this home, which the hostess remodeled herself, has three guest rooms. The hostess gathers the blueberries she bakes in her muffins, and she also hooks rugs on a loom in the living room. *Represented by:* Houseguests Cape Cod, Host Home #2, (617) 385-8332. $20–$30.

Forestdale. Almost entirely surrounded by trees and by ponds in which to swim, this home offers two guest rooms, which share a bath. The arrangement is ideal for a pair of couples traveling together. From the patio, where guests are invited to relax, one can see the sun set over the water. Sandwich, the Cape's oldest settlement, is nearby; and Falmouth, where you can catch a ferry to Nantucket or Martha's Vineyard, is a short drive away. *Represented by:* Houseguests Cape Cod, Host Home #2, (617) 385-8332. $35–$55.

Harwich Port. Two blocks from the beach and a short walk from many restaurants, this house has three rooms for guests. The guest room on the top floor used to be a sailmaker's loft. Guests returning from the beach are invited to shower and dress in an area beside the patio, which has a fountain around which breakfast is served. *Represented by:* Houseguests Cape Cod, Host Home #2, (617) 385-8332. $25–$40.

Marston Mills (the Boat House). A converted boat house suspended over a pond with a gaggle of geese, this accommodation has a boat-shaped kitchen and a large sun deck. The main house, plenty far away for privacy, has additional rooms for guests. *Represented by:* Houseguests Cape Cod, House Guest #3, (617) 385-8332. Weekly only; rates on request.

South Yarmouth (on the Bass River). This house, where guests are offered a welcoming evening cocktail, has five separate accommodations. One room has a private bath and cable TV, and a studio apartment, available by the week only, has a fireplace, a kitchenette, a cable TV, and a private patio. River beaches are a short walk away, and the hosts have boat and fishing gear that guests are invited to use. The house, once a farmhouse, is 10 minutes from Hyannis, which has a plethora of restaurants and night spots. A full country breakfast is served. *Represented by:* Houseguests Cape Cod, Host Home #s 1, 2, 3, 4, and 5, (617) 385-8332. $20; studio apartment $200 weekly.

Wellfleet. Not far from the docks of a typical New England fishing village, as well as the National Seashore, this home is directly on the water. Guests can fish or swim in any of twelve nearby ponds. The freshwater ponds in the Wellfleet area are warm, clean, and surrounded by trees. *Represented by:* Houseguests Cape Cod, Host Home #2, (617) 385-8332. $25–$35.

Yarmouth Port. The hostess, a busy professional woman, tells guests where her secret swimming spot is. The house is a weathered shingle cottage with a guest room that overlooks a bog and the ocean. *Represented by:* Houseguests Cape Cod, Host Home #2, (617) 385-8332. $38–$45.

Tree-lined Street. Shirley serves breakfast on her flagstone-floored, glass-enclosed terrace. Her living room has exposed-beam ceilings, a fireplace, and the kind of furnishings and appointments that obviously reflect the taste of someone thoroughly in touch with interior design. Located at the end of a tree-lined street, Shirley's house features guest quarters with a private entrance and bath. *Represented by:* New England Bed & Breakfast, (617) 244-2112. Rates on request.

Host Home #2 (*Houseguests Cape Cod*)

Concord **MASSACHUSETTS**

Hawthorne Inn

462 Lexington Road, Concord, MA 01742. (617) 369-5610.
Hosts: Gregory Burch and Marilyn Mudry.

The Hawthorne Inn is an 1870 Colonial structure on 1.5 acres of wooded land that was owned, in turn, by Nathaniel Hawthorne, Ralph Waldo Emerson, and the Alcott family. A pine tree Hawthorne planted still stands on the property, which is immediately across the road from the master's homesite. Recently George and Marilyn planted seven hundred spring-flowering bulbs around the goldfish pond. The grounds already boast numerous flowering trees and bushes and a vegetable garden.

The rooms, with hardwood floors covered by Oriental and rag rugs, are furnished with antiques. Original art works, ranging from antique Japanese ukiyo-e prints to contemporary sculpture, appear throughout the building. The rooms contain books of poetry, magazines, am-fm clock radios, and sometimes bowls of fruit and vases of freshly cut flowers.

Gregory and Marilyn serve a complimentary breakfast of home-baked breads, fresh fruit, juice, and tea, and their own special blend of coffee. In season, raspberries and grapes grown on the property show up on the breakfast table. The Hawthorne Inn is close to such treasures as Emerson's house, the Old North Bridge, and Walden Pond.

Accommodations: 6 rooms with shared bath. *Smoking:* Permitted in guest rooms only. *Children:* Permitted. *Pets:* Not permitted. *Breakfast:* Included. *Driving Instructions:* Located ¾ mile east of Concord's town square.

The Victorian

24 South Water Street, Edgartown, Massachusetts. *Mailing Address:* P.O. Box 947, Edgartown, MA 02539; off season: P.O. Box 251, Wilmington, VT 02363. (617) 627-4784; off season: (802) 464-3716. *Hosts:* Marilyn and Jack Kayner.

Although the back part of the Victorian was built in the early 1700s, the front part of the house was not completed until around 1820. The building is Victorian, with widow's-walk balconies off several of the rooms, and bay and dormer windows.

The guest rooms are furnished with antiques such as marble-topped dressers and tables and eighteenth-century canopied four-posters. Each guest room has a private bath, complete with extra-large towels, and decorator touches such as matching sheets and wallpaper characterize the rooms. Some rooms have views of the harbor, and Marilyn and Jack make sure that each guest room is stocked with fresh flowers and mints.

The sitting room, which has a color television set and a marble fireplace, is always available for use by guests, as is the enclosed lawn and garden area, where cocktails and conversation often precede dinner. In a breakfast room with a fireplace, Marilyn and Jack serve a complimentary breakfast.

Accommodations: 14 rooms with private bath. *Smoking:* Permitted. *Children:* Permitted during off season (November 2 through March 31) only; check in advance. *Pets:* Not permitted. *Breakfast:* Included. *Driving Instructions:* Take the ferry from Woods Hole, and then follow the signs to Edgartown.

Sea Gull Lodge

41 Belvidere Road, Falmouth, MA 02541. (617) 548-0679.
Hosts: John D. and Doris L. Gouliamas.

Situated on grounds planted with pines and maples, the Sea Gull is a 1948 Cape Cod structure with gables and shutters and a shaded front porch. The Sea Gull, operated by the Gouliamases since 1953, has a backyard patio with chaise lounges, and a picnic area complete with a brick-and-stone fireplace.

John and Doris own some genuine heirloom furniture: several antique Swedish pieces were hand-carved out of heavy oak as long ago as 1679. The living room has two davenports, six chairs, two coffee tables, and a large table—all of hand-carved oak. The walls are paneled with wide pine boards, and a fireplace warms the room in chilly weather. Several paintings and a wood sculpture hang on the living room walls, and the floor, its planks diagonally laid, is covered with a heavy area rug.

All the guest rooms have wood floors covered by small rugs, and cedar-lined closets. All rooms but one have television.

Doris and John don't serve breakfast but are more than happy to serve guests iced tea on the patio.

Accommodations: 2 rooms with shared bath. *Smoking:* Permitted. *Children:* Permitted. *Pets:* Not permitted. *Driving Instructions:* From Boston, take Route 28 to Scranton Avenue in Falmouth, then turn left on Lowry.

Schofield's Guest House

335 Grand Avenue, Falmouth Heights, MA 02540. (617) 548-4648. *Host:* Clyde E. Schofield.

Clyde, who's been in the guest-house business for twenty years, observed: "People are people no matter where you go." Clyde's matter-of-factness about the nature of travel and people hasn't deflected potential guests, who, he assures us, arrive after consulting with the Cape Cod Chamber of Commerce. "They just keep on sending them, and most of them keep coming back year after year because my rates are reasonable and I own a beautiful piece of the ocean."

Clyde has a large sundeck 100 feet from the ocean and facing it. His beach is a private one for guests only. "I don't need to be fancy, people who like the ocean like my place." Guests who want to may watch television in the lobby, with its numerous lounge chairs, which "shuts down automatically—at eleven."

The four guest rooms share two baths. Although Clyde doesn't serve breakfast, he says "There's food close enough."

Accommodations: 4 rooms with shared baths. *Smoking:* Permitted. *Children:* Permitted. *Pets:* Not permitted. *Driving Instructions:* Take Route 90 into Falmouth and stay on Main Street until you see the ocean; turn left, and keep your eyes open.

The Ellings' Guest House

R.D. 3, Box 6, Great Barrington, MA 01230. (413) 528-4103. *Hosts:* Ray and Josephine Elling.

A 1746 Colonial structure, The Ellings' Guest House was built by Stephen King, the owner of a woolen mill. The house is surrounded by cornfields, mountains, gardens, and a large lawn. Tall pines and maples shade the grounds, which feature a tree swing and badminton and horseshoe facilities.

Across the road, a river that runs through cornfields forms, at a bend, a swimming hole complete with a sandy beach. The central parlor (furnished, like the guest rooms, in antiques and Colonial reproductions) has a large fireplace and a writing desk that will please those who enjoy looking first at words they've put on paper, and then, an instant later, at a field of corn.

The guest rooms, two with private baths and four others sharing two baths, offer pretty views of cornfields or mountains or spreading lawns with gardens. Ray and Jo, who believe in privacy and in knocking before they enter rooms, serve a complimentary breakfast that usually consists of homemade muffins and jams, and all the coffee or tea you require.

Accommodations: 6 rooms, 2 with private bath. *Smoking:* Permitted. *Children:* Permitted. *Pets:* Not permitted. *Breakfast:* Included. *Driving Instructions:* On Route 23-41, a half mile west of Route 7 in Great Barrington.

Nantucket **MASSACHUSETTS**

Carlisle House

26 North Water Street, Nantucket, MA 02554. (617) 228-0720. *Hosts:* John and Susan Bausch.

Built in 1765, the Carlisle House is a large, typically New England structure with a sun porch and a shaded veranda. John and Susan have maintained the original appointments, which include wide pine floors and a number of fireplaces. Several guest rooms feature fireplaces, as does the living room, which is decorated with original artworks.

The Bausches serve a complimentary breakfast, weather permitting, on the sun porch, which has a cable color television set that guests are invited to watch. The veranda, shaded by trees and flowers and complete with summer furniture, is a place where, says Susan, guests may partake of everything from packed lunches to their favorite cocktails.

Accommodations: 13 rooms, 4 with private bath. *Smoking:* Permitted. *Children:* Over 9 permitted. *Pets:* Not permitted. *Breakfast:* Included. *Driving Instructions:* On Water Street, near the center of town.

The Chestnut House

3 Chestnut Street, Nantucket, MA 02554. (617) 228-0049.
Hosts: Jerry and Jeannette Carl.

"The wart," a term some Nantucketers use when they mean "cottage," didn't become an addition to the house until 1950, but the Chestnut House itself dates back to about 1856. A first addition appeared on the house in 1905, and the three-part structure strikes one now as rambling and roomy.

And friendly—Jerry and Jeannette Carl make a point of meeting all their guests personally. "This is one of our pleasures," as Jerry put it. Meeting guests always compels Jerry and Jeannette to hold forth on the idiosyncrasies of their cat, a Russian Blue with a will of iron (all attempts at feline reconditioning have failed miserably) who occupies room 11—whether guests like it or not. "So far it's working out," they say.

The Carls have five guest rooms with private baths and four others sharing two baths. The wart has a complete kitchen, a bedroom with a double bed, and a living room with a convertible sofa. Claudia, Jerry and Jeannette's daughter, makes by hand quilts that compliment the rugs her father hooks. Jeannette's paintings cover the walls: "Don't shudder," Jerry says, "she's good." (Her paintings are figurative, neo-impressionistic studies of flowers and animals and people.)

Accommodations: 9 rooms, 4 with private bath. *Smoking:* Permitted. *Children:* Over 5 permitted. *Pets:* Not permitted. *Driving Instructions:* Three blocks from the steamboat wharf.

Grieder Guest House

43 Orange Street, Nantucket, MA 02554. (617) 228-1399.
Hosts: Ruth and William Grieder.

It sometimes seems that every house in New England was owned by a whaling captain, but this one, built in the early 1700s, probably actually was. Orange Street used to be called the "street of captains," and appropriately enough, Ruth is a third-generation Nantucketer with sea captains on both sides of her family. William's father was once a lighthouse keeper on the island. They have been operating their guest house since 1952, and, in a tone suggesting understatement, Ruth says they "enjoy the business immensely."

The guest rooms have exposed beams on the ceilings, "ship's knees" in the corners, pineapple four-poster beds, sea chests, and braided rugs.

Ruth and William don't serve any meals, but their being in the center of Nantucket compensates for that—you can walk to a restaurant or the ocean. Picnic facilities in the shaded backyard are available for guests.

Accommodations: 2 rooms with shared bath. *Smoking:* Permitted. *Children:* Permitted. *Pets:* Not permitted. *Driving Instructions:* In the center of town, adjacent to Main Street.

House of the Seven Gables, Inc.

32 Cliff Road, Nantucket, MA 02554. (617) 228-4706. *Host:* Richard L. Branscombe.

The House of the Seven Gables, a large 1880s Victorian building with seven gables, is not the one immortalized by Nathaniel Hawthorne. This building originally served as the annex for one of Nantucket's oldest hotels, which was destroyed in 1972.

Several guest rooms have views of the Nantucket Harbor, and all are decorated with a combination of genuine antiques and period reproductions. The parlor, always available for guests to relax in, features a color television set.

Richard serves guests a complimentary breakfast of coffee or tea, juice, and freshly baked Danish. The house overlooks Nantucket Harbor and is a ten-minute walk from Main Street. It is open from June 14 through September 7.

Accommodations: 11 rooms, 8 with private bath. *Smoking:* Permitted. *Children:* Permitted sometimes (check in advance). *Pets:* Not permitted. *Breakfast:* Included. *Driving Instructions:* On Cliff Road about three blocks from Main Street.

Nantucket **MASSACHUSETTS**

Martin's Guest House

61 Centre Street, Nantucket, MA 02554. (617) 228-0678.
Hosts: Anne and Frank Berger.

Originally built in 1803 by a man Frank Berger refers to as a "mariner and gentleman," Martin's is a large, typically Nantucket structure with two gables on the roof and one over the doorway. The house has several fireplaces—one in the parlor for the use of guests and five more in the guest rooms, several of which are furnished with genuine antiques and period reproductions.

Minutes from downtown Nantucket and all its attractions, Martin's offers guests a large lawn and a complimentary Continental breakfast each morning, with homemade muffins and breads. Commenting on Nantucket's many attractions, Frank concludes that "mostly, Nantucket's meant for long, leisurely strolls along winding roads with rose-covered cottages, or along miles of open, unspoiled, clean beaches."

Accommodations: 13 rooms, 6 with private bath. *Smoking:* Permitted. *Children:* Permitted. *Pets:* Not permitted. *Breakfast:* Included. *Driving Instructions:* Near the center of town.

Nantucket Landfall

4 Harbor View Way, Nantucket, MA 02554. (617) 228-0500. *Hostess:* Dorothy M. Mortenson.

Built on the site of an old whaling business, the Nantucket Landfall is a 1928 Cape Cod structure with a porch tucked under an overhanging gable. Beside the porch is an old weathered fence that in the summer seems almost to be holding back the roses and hydrangeas that Dorothy grows. In June and July there are flowers everywhere.

Amid profuse shrubbery and flowers, Dorothy has managed to find room for a barbecue and a picnic table, which guests are invited to use. With the ocean right across the street, Dorothy's veranda offers nothing less than a panoramic view of Nantucket Harbor. She claims Nantucket's moors are "like Scotland's own."

Dorothy doesn't serve breakfast, but she helps her guests ease into the day by offering them coffee in the morning. She describes her place as informal, congenial, and comfortable. She quotes Conrad: "But if you have sighted it on the expected bearing, then the landfall is good."

Accommodations: 6 rooms, 4 with private bath. *Smoking:* Permitted. *Children:* Permitted. *Pets:* Not permitted. *Driving Instructions:* The center of town.

Royal Manor Guest House

31 Centre Street, Nantucket, MA 02554. (617) 228-0600. *Hosts:* Leon Macy Royal and Eleanor Jewett Royal.

Leon Macy Royal says the Royal Manor was one of the first houses built after the great Nantucket fire of 1846. He also says the house is one of Nantucket's best built, pointing to its 18- by 20-foot-high studded recessed windows with lovely panel work surrounding them and the wooden shutters on the inside. The house has elaborate cornice work and was constructed in the backplaster method (an inside and an outside wall of plaster, with 10 inches of airspace between them. It is on a 12,000-square-foot lot landscaped with shrubbery and trees, with a border of flowers. Its two porches, one open and one closed, are surrounded by flower boxes.

Each guest room has a fireplace with an Italian marble mantel, antique door knobs, an Oriental rug, and antique furnishings and fixtures.

The Royals have been operating the Royal Manor for thirty-seven years, and most of their guests, says Leon, are repeat lodgers or people recommended by them. Their confidence in satisfying guests is such that they don't even have a brochure. Leon and Eleanor don't serve any meals, but the Royal Manor is convenient to several good eating places.

Accommodations: 7 rooms, 5 with private bath. *Smoking:* Permitted. *Children:* Over 10 permitted. *Pets:* Not permitted. *Driving Instructions:* In the center of town.

The Benjamin Choate House

25 Tyng Street, Newburyport, MA 01950. (617) 462-4786.
Host: Herbert A. Fox.

Situated at the crest of Tyng Street (overlooking the Merrimack River, the boats tied up by Towle Silversmiths, and the North End Boat Club), the Benjamin Choate House is a three-story Federal structure. Several rooms in the house retain their original Indian shutters on the windows. The kitchen features antique paneling and the largest residential hearth in Newburyport.

Furnished with antiques, the beds made with hand-ironed designer sheets, the guest rooms feature Oriental rugs and an extensive collection of artwork that Mr. Fox accumulated during his twenty years as a master printer for such artists as Leonard Baskin, Saul Steinberg, and Joseph Albers. Mr. Fox's collection also includes many museum-quality old masters' prints.

Mr. Fox encourages his guests to join him in a glass of wine in front of one of the fireplaces, and provides wine and bar glasses for guests' private use. A full complimentary home-cooked breakfast is served each morning in the kitchen. Cloth napkins, antique lace tablecloth, and fresh flowers set the tone.

Accommodations: 5 rooms, 2 with private bath. *Smoking:* Permitted. *Children:* Permitted. *Pets:* Permitted, but check in advance. *Breakfast:* Included. *Driving Instructions:* Take Route I-95 to the exit for Newburyport onto Route 113; follow Route 113 for 1 1/2 miles; then turn left on Tyng Street.

Amherst House

38 Ocean Avenue, Oak Bluffs, MA 02557. (617) 693-3430.
Hosts: Marna Bunce and Dick Konicek.

Situated next to a park on Martha's Vineyard and directly facing the ocean, Amherst House is an 1869 Victorian structure. It was owned for years by a wealthy Philadelphia family, the daughter of which, the locals say, was a recluse who had her birds flown up to spend the summer with her. When Dick Konicek bought the house, he discovered an elaborate collection of fancy hats, some still with price stickers, that guests can see in the Hat Room. He also came across a great deal of wicker furniture and several Oriental rugs. The decor throughout Amherst House is a combination of wicker and wood, with Oriental rugs here and there. The house contains, as Dick puts it, "no plastic."

A specialist in the hard sciences, Dick teaches at the University of Massachusetts School of Education; Marna, his partner, teaches at the Pelham elementary school. Each morning, they serve guests a complimentary breakfast with Marna's home-baked breads (she gets up early to bake them).

A special treat the Amherst House offers: good seats for the concerts that take place each Sunday evening (in season) in the park next door.

Accommodations: 4 rooms, 1 with private bath. *Smoking:* Permitted in lounge only. *Children:* Permitted. *Pets:* Not permitted. *Breakfast:* Included. *Driving Instructions:* On Ocean Park, near the dock of the Woods Hole ferry and the bandstand.

The Oak House

Seaview and Pequot Avenue, Box 299, Oak Bluffs, MA 02557. (617) 693-4187. *Hosts:* Marcia and Stuart Haley.

This 1872 Queen Anne structure on Martha's Vineyard was built, as its name implies, of oak. In 1876 Governor Claflin, who owned it then, added wide porches as well as leaded glass (some with stained-glass trim) in more than fifty-five windows. The bathrooms have tin walls and ceilings, and many original marble sinks and fixtures still remain.

Five guest rooms have balconies, and several have views of Cape Cod or the ocean. A number have antique beds, some have intricate oak paneling, one has open-beamed ceilings, and another has an ocean view interrupted handsomely by a window whose top is stained glass. Antique furnishings and lovely woodwork appear in most guest rooms. The Haleys' living room, spacious and furnished with some antiques, has a grand piano and an electric organ.

Marcia and Stuart do not serve breakfast but do offer their guests coffee each morning on a sun porch overlooking the ocean.

Accommodations: 10 rooms with shared bath. *Smoking:* Permitted. *Children:* Discouraged. *Pets:* Not permitted. *Driving Instructions:* Two blocks south of the Oak Bluffs Steamship Dock.

Asheton House

3 Cook Street, Provincetown, MA 02657. (617) 487-9966.
Hosts: Jim Bayard and Les Schaufler.

Asheton House consists of two early-nineteenth-century houses (1806 and 1840) erected by the Cook family, which owned a fleet of whaling vessels. The grounds feature Japanese temple trees, a semiformal English boxwood garden, and sundecks that overlook Cape Cod Bay. The sunsets of the bay fall, say Jim and Les, into the never-to-be-forgotten category. So does their collection of antiques.

One guest room, furnished with period French pieces, has a fireplace, a view of the bay, and a large private bath. Another room, overlooking the garden, is done in natural wicker and bamboo. There is also a three-room apartment with a living room, a bedroom, and a spacious kitchen–dining area (complete with washer and dryer).

To prepare you for exploring Provincetown's shopping areas or its vast expanse of dunes, Jim and Les serve a complimentary breakfast.

Accommodations: 8 rooms, 2 with private bath. *Smoking:* Permitted. *Children:* Not permitted. *Pets:* Not permitted. *Breakfast:* Included. *Driving Instructions:* Proceeding north on Route 6, take the first left after the town line; go to the water and turn right; then go half a mile.

Rockport **MASSACHUSETTS**

Eden Pines Inn

Eden Road, Rockport, MA 01966. (617) 546-2505. *Hostess:* Inge Sullivan.

The Eden Pines Inn—a large shuttered and shingled New England structure with an upper porch and a brick sundeck—borders directly on the ocean. For those more inclined toward smooth old rocks than chaise lounges, huge boulders begin where the sundeck ends. The view from both is spectacular—lobstermen and ocean liners and the famous twin lighthouses of Thatcher's Island.

The view during Inge Sullivan's complimentary breakfast, with Scandinavian pastries, is also marvelous, especially to those who enjoy seeing the rim of the ocean's horizon over the rims of their coffee cups.

All guest rooms have a private bath and a sitting area. Two rooms feature private decks, and of the six rooms, only one lacks an ocean view. The parlor has a fireplace, books, and a television set. Inge serves tea at 3 P.M., and at 5 P.M. glasses and ice are set out for guests, who may store beverages in a conveniently located refrigerator.

Inge also has a cottage for rent on Bearskin Neck, a strip of land with outstanding views of Rockport Harbor.

Accommodations: 6 rooms with private bath. *Smoking:* Permitted. *Children:* Young children not permitted (check first). *Pets:* Not permitted. *Breakfast:* Included. *Driving Instructions:* Take Route 128 North; turn left onto Route 127, then right onto Route 127A and go a mile. The inn is on the left.

Rockport **MASSACHUSETTS**

Lantana House

22 Broadway, Rockport, MA 01966. (617) 546-3535. *Hosts:* Cyndie and Larry Sewell.

The Lantana House, which Cyndie Sewell reckons at about 150 years old, is almost directly in the middle of Rockport. Through the windows on one side of the house you can see Saint Mary's Episcopal Church, slightly obscured by trees in the summer; and from the staircase's landing window you can see the docks area and the ocean beyond it. An art gallery on the ground floor beneath the building's porch is where Cyndie and Larry hope to have this year, as they did last year, a resident artist working and selling his wares.

The Sewells' living room is decorated with paintings, primarily watercolor seascapes, and furnished with dark walnut traditional pieces covered in a green velvety material. Cyndie is proud of the rooms' numerous objets d'art and is especially pleased with an aluminum sculpture that sits in the living room.

Cyndie and Larry serve a Continental breakfast of juice, coffee, rolls, and homemade muffins. When it's warm, guests usually prefer having breakfast on the sundeck.

Accommodations: 8 rooms, 6 with private bath. *Smoking:* Permitted. *Children:* Permitted. *Pets:* Permitted. *Breakfast:* Included. *Driving Instructions:* From Boston, take Route 128 to its end, then turn left onto Route 127; the guest house is two blocks from the five-corner intersection in Rockport.

Seacrest Manor

131 Marmion Way, Rockport, MA 01966. (617) 546-2211. *Hosts:* Leighton T. Saville and Dwight B. MacCormack. Closed January.

An early nineteenth-century Colonial structure to which an eastern wing and a sun deck were added in the 1960s, Seacrest Manor is on a rocky Cape Anne crag. The view from the sun deck is extraordinary, encompassing almost 180 degrees. The strong of sight can discern Mount Agamenticus, 40 miles away in Maine. Straitsmouth Island, with its picturesque house and light, and the famous twin lights of Thatcher's Island are both easily visible from the sun deck.

Inside, the library, which includes several hundred volumes, has leather wing chairs, gray walls, a white door and ceiling moldings, and a fireplace. The living room, where afternoon tea is served, has a Colonial chandelier, a couch in front of a large window overlooking the garden, and a set of Colonial chairs.

The guest rooms are furnished with a combination of antiques and contemporary pieces. Some of these rooms have solid-wood doors, all are carpeted, and several afford ocean views. The rooms also feature fresh bouquets of flowers, turned-down beds with mints left on the pillows, a morning paper waiting outside the door, and if you remembered to leave them in the hall, your shoes freshly polished.

Leighton and Dwight serve a full breakfast, and when it's cold the dining room's hearth has a fire to warm things up. Seacrest Manor is closed in January.

Accommodations: 8 rooms, 4 with private bath. *Smoking:* Permitted. *Children:* Under 16 not permitted. *Pets:* Not permitted. *Breakfast:* Included. *Driving Instructions:* From Rockport Center, take Route 127A (Mount Pleasant Street) south; Marmion Way is the second left after the Delmar Nursing Home.

The Seafarer Guest House

86 Marmion Way, Rockport, MA 01966. (617) 546-6248.
Hosts: Mary and Gerry Pepin.

The Seafarer Guest House is an 1893 gambrel-roofed structure with column-supported porches formed by the roof's overhangs. The guest house, originally constructed to be part of a planned summer colony, was almost immediately incorporated into the Straitsmouth Inn complex of buildings.

The Seafarer, at the western edge of Gap Cove, is surrounded by the ocean, and each guest room has an ocean view. Mary and Gerry, intent on capturing a feeling of the sea, have scoured about and found many maritime ships' fittings, salvage pieces, and reproductions. Brass fittings, brass and teak towel racks, ships' lamps, and many kinds of nautical paraphernalia are found all over the house.

Each guest room has at least three original oil paintings by local artists; two of the rooms, both on the third floor, have kitchenettes, breakfast nooks, and private baths. A large old-fashioned porch leads into the living–sitting room, which has a fireplace, lovely antique furnishings, plenty of books and magazines, and a stereo that usually softly plays classical or contemporary music. Over the living room's fireplace is a large painting of a ship; other paintings hang in the hall and on all the landings.

Mary and Gerry serve a complimentary breakfast that includes, as well as juice and coffee, cranberry nutbread. The Seafarer is open from April 1 through November 15.

Accommodations: 8 rooms, 6 with private bath. *Smoking:* Permitted. *Children:* Small children not permitted (check first). *Pets:* Not permitted. *Breakfast:* Included. *Driving Instructions:* Take Route 127 North to Rockport Center, then take Route 127A for a mile to Marmion Way.

Sheffield **MASSACHUSETTS**

Ivanhoe Country House

Route 41, Sheffield, MA 01257. (413) 229-2143. *Hosts:* Carol and Dick Moghery.

The Ivanhoe Country House is a large 1780 New England farmhouse located between the foot of Mount Race and the shores of Berkshire Lake (its guest rooms overlook either one or the other). The 25-acre grounds contain, in addition to the splendid Berkshire landscape, a lighted sleighing slope and a swimming pool.

The parlor—called the Chestnut Room because of its wood paneling—features a fireplace, a library, a color television set, and a Ping-Pong and other game tables. Three of the nine guest rooms have working fireplaces, two have kitchenette units (refrigerators are available to guests who bring perishables or wine and spirits).

The Mogherys include a complimentary Continental breakfast (muffins and coffee, tea, or cocoa), which they serve at your bedroom door. The house is convenient to Butternut ski basin, the Appalachian Trail, Tanglewood, and the Jacob's Pillow dance festival.

Accommodations: 9 rooms, 6 with private bath. *Smoking:* Permitted. *Children:* Permitted. *Pets:* Dogs permitted. *Breakfast:* Included. *Driving Instructions:* Located 7 miles south of Great Barrington on Route 41.

Haven Guest House

P.O. Box 1022, Vineyard Haven, MA 02568. (617) 693-3333. *Hosts:* Karl and Lynn Buder.

The Haven Guest House—architecturally something of a classic American bungalow with a neo-Williamsburg interior—was built in 1918 as a wedding present for one of the Colgate daughters and accommodated guests at the Colgate estate. The house, just outside a Martha's Vineyard town, is near the summer homes of William Styron, Art Buchwald, and Lillian Hellman.

Each guest room has a private bath and a sitting area, and two have private decks. Furnishings vary from room to room, as do the predominant woods several rooms are named for: There are The Walnut, The Mahogany, The Oak, and The Maple rooms. Decor includes Victorian, Colonial, and Art Deco; eclecticism is more the rule than the exception.

The public areas of the house include an unusually large foyer and central staircase, a living room with a fireplace, and a sunny screened-in porch where guests partake of a morning paper and a complimentary breakfast with homemade breads and muffins.

Accommodations: 9 rooms with private bath. *Smoking:* Permitted in guest rooms only. *Children:* Over 12 permitted. *Pets:* Not permitted. *Breakfast:* Included. *Driving Instructions:* From Falmouth, follow signs for Woods Hole ferry (advance auto reservations required).

Victorian Tourist and Antiques House

120 Main Street, Williamstown, MA 01267. (413) 458-3121. *Hostess:* Mary L. Dempsey.

The original 1780 Colonial structure was moved to this location in 1820, when an additional building was erected. These two adjoining houses first served as the Williams College infirmary. The house was renovated in 1917 by Francis Sayre and his wife, President Woodrow Wilson's daughter. While in office, the president visited here often.

When Mary Dempsey bought the house, the blackberries were growing in through the windows, but she revitalized it with the objects of her profession—antiques. The parlor has a fireplace made of green stone, a rosewood Chippendale sofa upholstered in a red print fabric, a maroon and burgundy Oriental rug, hardwood oaken floors and two French doors leading onto a maple-shaded porch. The dining room has a Chinese blue Oriental rug, Chippendale chairs, and a grand old grandfather clock. The kitchen has an old hutch with a display of teapots. The guest rooms are also furnished with Mary's antiques, and most of them feature four-poster beds.

The front yard is dominated by a large maple tree, and the east side of the house is obscured by a number of them. Leo, Mary's 175-pound German shepherd, roams the property, which is adjacent to Williams College.

Accommodations: 8 rooms sharing 3 baths. *Smoking:* Permitted. *Children:* Permitted. *Pets:* Small pets permitted (check first). *Driving Instructions:* On Main Street in the center of Williamstown.

Wellman General Store Guest Apartment

205 Main Street, Horton, Michigan. *Mailing Address:* P.O. Box 58, Horton, MI 49246. (517) 563-2231. *Hostess:* Karen D. Gauntlet.

This 1886 brick structure, listed in Michigan's Historic Registry, used to be a general store. When the wreckers were just about ready to tear it down, Karen Gauntlet threw down the gauntlet, restored the building, and opened her doors to guests.

Karen has one guest accommodation—an apartment. The

bedroom used to be a storage area for canned goods; the kitchen once served as a meat cooler; and years ago the bathroom functioned as a post office.

Karen, an interior designer by trade, decorated her guest apartment with wall-to-wall carpeting, a leather card table and chairs, a sofa and rocker, and a color television set. The apartment features antique artwork and appointments, and a shell collection. It has two private entrances—one in front and one in the rear garden.

Karen doesn't serve breakfast but for an additional charge will stock the apartment's refrigerator with juice, eggs, sausages, fresh bread, Colombian coffee, and fruit and cheese. For a charge, she will serve dinner, which might include beef bourguignon with potatoes amandine and carrots Grand Marnier.

Accommodations: 1 apartment with private bath. *Smoking:* Permitted. *Children:* One or two permitted, but only in apartment with parents. *Pets:* Not permitted. *Breakfast:* Food for preparation by guests provided for an additional charge. *Driving Instructions:* Take Route 60 to Spring Arbor Road, then take Moscow Road South to the village of Horton; turn right on Main Street.

Blue Earth. This downtown accommodation is a two-room efficiency apartment with a private bath and a small refrigerator. The room has twin beds, but the hosts allow larger parties who don't object to sleeping bags. *Represented by:* The International Spareroom, MN-64, (714) 755-3194. $9.75–$13.00.

Blue Earth. This guest house can accommodate a family of seven. The hosts, a farmer and a teacher, will gladly arrange farm tours, and the area contains many antique shops. *Represented by:* The International Spareroom, MN-63, (714) 755-3194. $13.00–$19.50.

Lake Nakomis (Minneapolis Area). This guest house within blocks of Lake Nakomis has a large yard where guests may relax. The area has many parks, as well as several lakes. *Represented by:* The Bed & Breakfast League, Ltd., (202) 232-8718. $20–$28.

Lake of Isles (Minneapolis Area). This guest house has a greenhouse and a gazebo, as well as a convenient location: The Walker Art Center, the Guthrie Theatre, and shopping and restaurants are close by. *Represented by:* The Bed & Breakfast League, Ltd., (202) 232-8718. $30–$38.

St. Louis Park (Minneapolis Area). Open to families traveling with children, this guest house features a fireplace and a library stocked with books and games. The hosts make a canoe and a bicycle available to guests, and their home is only a block from the bus. *Represented by:* The Bed & Breakfast League, Ltd., (202) 232-8718. $30–$38.

The Burn

712 North Union Street, Natchez, MS 39120. (601) 445-8566. *Hosts:* Buzz and Bobbie Harper.

An 1832 Greek Revival structure with four Doric columns and a paneled doorway surrounded by five glass insets, The Burn is beautifully appointed. One guest room features hand-carved Prudent Mallard furniture, an Aubusson carpet, a chandelier, and an elaborate fireplace with a huge gilt-framed mirror on its mantel. Another guest room has an acanthus carved bed and dressing table, two wing-chairs upholstered in a tufted gray fabric, a fireplace, a circular gilt-framed wide-angle mirror complete with an eagle, and elaborate valenced curtains in the same fabric draped over the four-poster bed.

The music room features laminated and carved Belter furniture (a love seat and several chairs covered in a tufted gold fabric), a crystal chandelier, a large gilt-framed mirror on the fireplace mantel, a large classical painting, and a harp. The entrance hall is furnished with New York Empire pieces, a brass and crystal chandelier, a wide-angle gilt-framed mirror with an eagle perched on top, several Oriental rugs and a large, sinuous spiral staircase with two eighteenth-century Mannerist paintings halfway up it. The Harpers offer a complimentary breakfast.

Accommodations: 6 rooms with private bath. *Smoking:* Permitted. *Children:* Over 6 permitted. *Pets:* Not permitted. *Breakfast:* Included (dinner on request). *Driving Instructions:* Take Route 61 to Great River Road, and take North Union Street next. The Burn is on North Union between Bee and Oak streets.

Old Pioneer Garden

Unionville 79, Imlay, NV 89418. (702) 538-7585. *Hosts:* Mitzi and Lew Jones.

One way to avoid the pressure of keeping up with the Joneses is to live in a ghost town, which is exactly what Mitzi and Lew Jones decided to do. The Old Pioneer Garden is a genuine ghost town, which Mitzi and Lew have been restoring for themselves and their guests.

The main farmhouse was built in 1861, when mining for silver, gold, antimony, and copper attracted prospectors and businessmen to the area. The old Arizona mine, which virtually made the town of Unionville, is a short walk from the property. The grounds are bound to please nature lovers—there are a trout stream, a pond, and spectacular mountain views. The elevation here is 6,000 feet plus; from the farmhouse porches one can view the fruit trees and animals and the snow-covered mountains in the distance.

The Joneses raise sheep, goats, pigs, chickens, geese, guineas, and ducks. "We raise much of what we eat," says Mitzi. They're more than generous when it comes time to feed the guests. Their rates include a full ranch-style breakfast.

Accommodations: 5 rooms, 1 with private bath. *Smoking:* Tolerated. *Children:* Permitted. *Pets:* Permitted if well behaved. *Breakfast:* Included. *Driving Instructions:* From Winnemucca take Route 1-80 south to Mill City; take Route 400 south for 16 miles, then turn right on the gravel road and go 3 miles.

Cheney House Bed and Breakfast

40 Highland Street, Ashland, NH 03217. (603) 968-7968.
Hosts: Mike and Daryl Mooney.

Situated on 3.5 acres planted with maple, catalpa, spruce, and butternut trees, Cheney House is an 1895 Victorian brick structure, its upper stories painted beige. The entrance foyer, which is rather the centerpiece of the house, has oaken floors and wainscoting, stained-glass windows, and a carved oaken balustrade. Breakfast is served in this foyer and consists of such items as oven pancakes stuffed with poached eggs, bacon, or sausage, or perhaps homemade blueberry pancakes with real maple syrup.

The guest rooms are decorated with country furniture. One has an antique handmade quilt covering a queen-size bed, dark brown wall-to-wall carpeting, Currier and Ives prints on the walls, and a window overlooking the lawns and garden. All of the guest rooms have views of lawn, flowers, and trees.

Cheney House is within walking distance of a Squam Lake beach and tennis courts.

Accommodations: 3 rooms with shared bath. *Smoking:* Permitted. *Children:* Permitted. *Pets:* Not permitted. *Breakfast:* Included. *Driving Instructions:* From I-93 North exit at Ashland, bear left at Cumberland Farms, and take the first left onto Highland Street.

Cannon Mountain Inn

Route 116, Franconia, NH 03580. (603) 823-9574. *Host:* Gerald A. Kasch.

In case you feel like flying here, make sure you can set down on Gerald's 3,000-foot landing strip, which all things considered, doesn't take up too much of his property. In addition to the landing strip, the grounds, which consist of some 200 acres, also contain two soccer fields, a swimming hole, and a brook with trout.

Although the Cannon Mountain Inn has been a guest house since the days of horses and buggies, Gerald has only been its host for the past forty-five years or so. The inn features a fantastic view of the justifiably famous Franconia Notch, and the base of the Tucker Brook Ski Trail is in Gerald's front yard.

In addition to the nine guest rooms in the main house, Gerald offers guests a duplex cottage, each of whose floors features a combination bedroom and living room, a kitchenette, and a private bath.

There is no lack of things to do at and near the Cannon Mountain Inn. You can walk to the Robert Frost Museum or, without leaving the grounds, fish, hunt, ski, or play shuffleboard, croquet, or badminton.

Gerald takes pride in the fact that his guests return year after year.

Accommodations: 11 rooms, 3 with private bath. *Smoking:* Permitted. *Children:* Permitted. *Pets:* Permitted. *Driving Instructions:* Cannon Mountain is on Route 116, 2.5 miles from the center of Franconia.

The Grayhurst

11 F Street, Hampton Beach, NH 03842. (603) 926-2584.

Hosts: Peter and Judy Chaput.

Eighty feet from the ocean, the Grayhurst is an 1890 gambrel-roofed Cape Cod–style structure with porches on the first and second floors and a 40-foot row of flowers in front of it. The front yard and the 3-foot deep flower boxes on the porch are filled with petunias, geraniums, and marigolds. Old-time residents of the area remember one of the house's former residents—an opera singer who on Sunday mornings took up a position on a porch and burst into high-volume song. That porch overlooks the ocean and always gets a cool breeze.

From May through October Peter and Judy Chaput offer several efficiency apartments that feature private baths, television, and complete cooking facilities, as well as a cottage with 3 rooms and a private porch. The rooms are simply furnished.

One apartment has a nonworking fireplace with a hundred-year-old 3- by 4-foot seascape hanging above it, wall-to-wall carpeting, an antique oaken bureau, antique oaken chairs, and tasseled Colonial curtains.

Peter, who has a master's degree in business, currently teaches business and accounting courses at New Hampshire College.

The Grayhurst is in the center of Hampton Beach, which has numerous attractions. Guests are offered coffee and doughnuts.

Accommodations: 15 rooms, 4 with private bath. *Smoking:* Permitted. *Children:* Permitted. *Pets:* Not permitted. *Driving Instructions:* The Grayhurst is in the center of the beach area.

Stone Fox Lodge

Tine Mine Road, Box 406, Jackson, NH 01581. (203) 383-6636. *Hosts:* Ed and Alice Bannon.

Built around 1880 as a summer home, Stone Fox is a Victorian shingled structure with rock pillars and foundation. Legend has it that a friendly ghost named Murphy inhabits the house, but you're more likely to be awed by the natural beauty of the house's setting than worried by any of its supernatural denizens. The views from the guest rooms and the building's wraparound porch are nothing less than spectacular: One looks across Mount Washington and sees the Presidential Range of the White Mountains.

The living room has a large stone fireplace, antique wooden paneling, and Oriental rugs, both on the floors and displayed on the walls. Off the living room are two dining rooms with pine paneling and fireplaces. There are green plants in these rooms and nearly all the others.

The guest rooms are furnished with a combination of antique and 1930s and 1940s pieces, and on the landing leading to the rooms is a miniature John Thomas grandfather clock. Some of the guest rooms have Oriental rugs, and the halls and the bathrooms contain many green plants.

The lodge has a restaurant that serves meals to the public by reservation only, and Ed and Alice put out tea and cakes for their guests. The restaurant features entrées such as Cinnamon duck, Stone Fox steak, veal Bosco, and Chateaubriand for two.

The lodge is closed in April and May and from the end of the fall-foliage season through Christmas.

Accommodations: 5 rooms with shared bath. *Smoking:* Permitted. *Children:* Young ones discouraged. *Pets:* Check in advance. *Breakfast:* Included. *Driving Instructions:* Take Route 16B into Jackson, and turn up Tin Mine Road at the sign for the Tyrol Ski Area and the Stone Fox Lodge.

1895 House

74 Pleasant Street, Littleton, NH 03561. (603) 444-5200 or (609) 652-8634. *Hostess:* Susanne Watkins.

Built in the year of its name, 1895 House is a white Victorian structure with green shutters and a wraparound porch. The building is situated on half an acre of land, planted with sugar maples and 20-foot lilac bushes. The backyard of 1895 House is contiguous with a park that has a baseball diamond, tennis courts, and, close to the house, a gazebo.

A massive oak door with beveled glass insets opens into a foyer that has an oaken floor and hand-carved woodwork on the walls. The stairway leading upstairs is also made of oak, and its bannister posts were carved by hand.

The living room has sliding oaken doors with brass knobs, a Chippendale camelback couch upholstered in silver gray velvet, two Queen Anne chairs, and a tan, beige, and coral Oriental rug. The room has bay windows that overlook the porch and the town of Littleton, and the walls are hung with Oriental prints, such as original Japanese woodcuts, from Susanne's collection. The living room has a stereo, on which Susanne plays classical music. (Beethoven and Bach are two of her favorite composers, and she takes particular delight in the playing of Vladimir Horowitz.)

A pair of sliding oaken doors lead to the dining room, which has a brick fireplace with a carved oaken mantel incorporating a mirror inset and the head of Old Man Winter in bas-relief, an oaken dining table with rope legs, and a set of bay windows that overlook the high lilac bushes.

The guest rooms have oaken floors, oaken armoires and dressers, braided and Oriental rugs, quilts that Susanne made by hand, and Priscilla tieback curtains. The third floor guest rooms have slanted walls.

Accommodations: 6 rooms, 1 with private bath. *Smoking:* Permitted except in dining area. *Children:* Permitted. *Pets:* Sometimes permitted—check in advance. *Driving Instructions:* From I-91 take Route 302 east into Littleton, then turn left off Main Street onto Pleasant Street.

The Willows Inn

Box 527, Peterborough, NH 03458. (603) 924-3746. *Hosts:* Bob and Micheline Abbott.

Built in 1850, the Willows Inn was originally part of a large dairy before it became a guest house. (During the late 1930s, the two sisters who managed the guest house then charged $1.75 per night, dinner included.) The house, surrounded by spacious lawns with trees, is set back about 200 yards from the road.

The reception room is simply but comfortably furnished with Colonial antiques and reproduction pieces, wall-to-wall carpeting, a hand-hooked rug, several easy chairs, and a color television set.

The guest rooms, which have either twin or double beds, are furnished with a combination of Colonial antiques and reproduction pieces. They have maple floors, reproduction Colonial wallpapers, handmade Colonial curtains, and—in season—fresh flowers from the Abbotts' garden.

Bob and Micheline serve a Continental breakfast that includes juice, home-baked breads and Danishes, homemade jams and jellies, and coffee and tea.

Though small, the town of Peterborough hosts a number of cultural activities. The Peterborough Players and the American Stage Festival provide the town with theater each summer, and various music groups appear each season (the Monadnock Symphony Orchestra, Apple Hill Chamber Players, Concord Chamber Group, and Monadnock Chorale). Peterborough also has swimming and tennis facilities.

Accommodations: 14 rooms, 2 with private bath. *Smoking:* Permitted. *Children:* Permitted. *Pets:* Not permitted. *Breakfast:* Included. *Driving Instructions:* From Brattleboro take Route 9 east into Keene, then take Route 101 to Peterborough. The inn is 200 yards from Route 101.

Conover's Bay Head Inn

646 Main Avenue, Bay Head, NJ 08742. (201) 892-4664.
Hosts: Carl and Beverly Conover.

Bay Head, situated at the beginning of the inland waterway to Florida, was a resort as far back as the sixteenth-century, when the Leni-Lenape Indians summered here. Conover's Bay Head Inn is a large, shingled 1910 cottage-style structure with several small gables on its roof. The grounds, planted with geraniums and azaleas, contain a picnic area that guests may use.

The living room has a white stone fireplace with an antique walnut clock on its mantel, beige Bargello-pattern carpeting, a walnut couch upholstered in a dark beige fabric and brightened with needlepoint throw pillows, which Beverly made, and a mahogany table. The room is filled with plants.

One guest room has a bed with a lacy canopy and a matching spread, a chandelier with a Tiffany shade in greens and yellows, and a hand-painted night table. The third-floor guest rooms have dormer windows, and two of them have water views. One third-floor room, which has a vew of the Bay, has a huge Victorian bed and a delicate buttercup wallpaper that matches the pillows and the bedspread. Each guest room is color-coordinated, with matching wallpaper, pillows, and spreads. The guest rooms are further enhanced by doilies Beverly crocheted herself. One room reflects Carl's preoccupation with steam engines (he used to own one) and is decorated with all manner of gauges.

Carl and Beverly serve their guests complimentary wine, as well as a Continental breakfast that includes fresh-baked breads, which Beverly varies from day to day. The inn is open from February 15 through December 15.

Accommodations: 12 rooms, 2 with private bath. *Smoking:* Permitted. *Children:* Well-behaved older children permitted. *Pets:* Not permitted. *Breakfast:* Included. *Driving Instructions:* Take the Garden State Parkway to exit 98, pick up Routes 34 and 35 South, and continue to Point Pleasant Beach. Bay Head is the next town.

The Abbey

Columbia Avenue and Gurney Street, Cape May, NJ 08204. (609) 884-4506. *Hosts:* Jay and Marianne Shatz.

The Abbey was built in 1869 by a wealthy coal baron and politician, a man who doubtless cherished spectacular views. The city of Cape May and the Atlantic Ocean seem almost to have been designed for viewing from the Abbey's Tower Room high in the structure's 60-foot tower.

Stenciled and ruby-glass arched windows, 12-foot mirrors, fireplaces, carved walnut beds, marble-topped dressers—appointments like these are found throughout the Abbey. Jay and Marianne Shatz have assembled a stunning collection of ornate gas-lighting fixtures, which run on electricity these days and seem to show up in every room.

The back parlor features a slate fireplace with a huge gilt-framed mirror rising from its mantel, an 1840 Swiss harp made of mahogany and fruitwood, a heavily tufted green velvet parlor set carved out of walnut and inlaid with rosewood and tulip wood, ornate frieze wallpaper bordering the multicolored ceiling molding, and white-curtained bay windows. All of the fourth-floor guest rooms have private baths and small refrigerators. "I couldn't find any Victorian refrigerators," Marianne claims. The other guest rooms share a 15- by 15- foot bathroom with an Oriental Rug, a claw-foot tub, a pedestal sink and a brass chandelier.

Both Jay and Marianne have marketing backgrounds in the chemical industry, and they opened The Abbey in a spirit of elegant revenge—they had both stayed in too many motels.

Accommodations: 7 rooms, 4 with private bath. *Smoking:* Permitted but no cigars. *Children:* Over 12 permitted if well behaved. *Pets:* Not permitted. *Breakfast:* Included. *Driving Instructions:* Take the Garden State Parkway to its end, turn left on Ocean Street, then left again on Columbia Avenue.

The Brass Bed Victorian Guest House

719 Columbia Avenue, Cape May, NJ 08204. (609) 884-8075. *Hosts:* John and Donna Dunwoody.

So named because each guest room has one, The Brass Bed is an 1872 Gothic Revival structure. As John and Donna Dunwoody restored the old house they came across a good deal of dusty furniture that had obviously belonged to the original owner: His name appeared on shipping tags still attached to it.

The house has a 32-foot porch with white wicker furniture and long-backed rocking chairs fashioned of long-grained pine. The garden's flowers—two groupings of coleus and a mix of geraniums and begonias—complement the colors of the house: gold, sand, and chocolate brown.

The central parlor—where guests read, talk, or cajole John Dunwoody into playing his rosewood Graphola—has 12-foot French doors; an 1840 drop-leaf oaken desk with a 1900 Corona typewriter perched on it; a spoon-carved Lady Eastlake platform rocker; and an Indian rug with an abstract design in oranges and

blues. The hall and dining room have ornate plaster ceiling medallions, and a curved mahogany banister leads up to the second floor. The Congress Hall room features a blue Oriental rug with a floral pattern in golds, creams, and browns, an 1872 poplar armoire, and a late-nineteenth-century mahogany leaf table.

John and Donna serve a complimentary breakfast of fresh fruit, juices, cereal, coffee, and cake.

Accommodations: 8 rooms, 2 with private bath. *Smoking:* Not permitted in parlor or dining room. *Children:* Over 12 permitted. *Pets:* Not permitted. *Breakfast:* Included. *Driving Instructions:* Take the Garden State Parkway south to its end, turn left on Ocean Street, then left again on Columbia Avenue.

Captain Mey's Inn

202 Ocean Street, Cape May, NJ 08204. (609) 884-7793.
Hostesses: Carin Feddermann and Milly Laconfora.

This 1890 Victorian structure, built by a homeopathic physician, is named after Cornelius J. Mey, the founder of the Cape May community. "'Tis better to govern by love and friendship than by force," said he.

Carin and Milly, who do things like commission analyses to determine the original paint color of their house, furnished Captain Mey's Inn with stunning antiques. The parlor has a Gothic bookcase hand-carved out of dark oak; a lighter shade of hand-carved oak encircles the Tiffany stained glass and matching-shell-design tiles incorporated into the vestibule. The living room has a leaded-glass bay window, complete with a window seat, chestnut oak paneling, and a crowned, molded ceiling, as well as a fireplace.

The guest rooms tend to contain marble-topped dressers, 5-foot high and 200-year-old beds (some of oak and some of walnut), lace curtains, handmade quilts and afghans, Oriental carpets, and freshly cut flowers.

As do many people with taste, Carin and Milly play Mozart during breakfast, which they serve, idiosyncratically, by candlelight.

Accommodations: 10 rooms, 3 with private bath. *Smoking:* Permitted. *Children:* Over 12 permitted. *Pets:* Not permitted. *Breakfast:* Included. *Driving Instructions:* Take the Garden State Parkway to the Cape May exit; cross the bridge to Lafayette Street and go straight to the second red light; make a left onto Ocean Street.

The Dormer House International

800 Columbia Avenue, Cape May, NJ 08204. (609) 884-7446. *Hosts:* Bill and Peg Madden.

An 1895 Colonial Revival structure, the Dormer House was originally the private home of a Philadelphia marble dealer. The house, which the U.S. Navy used as a rehabilitation center between 1918 and 1920, has been a guest house for well over half a century. It was converted into apartments in the early 1970s. The house features a large front porch with a glassed-in area, and period furniture, including marble pieces, typifies the decor.

All the guest apartments, some of which are available only on a weekly basis, are fully equipped, although Bill and Peg don't supply linens (towels, sheets, pillowcases, etc.), maid service or breakfast.

One apartment, which accommodates six, has glass doors that open onto a private porch, a kitchen separated from the living room by an island counter with a maple butcher-block top, and a bedroom with two exposures. Some apartments have private entrances; some have rooms with three exposures; one has a fireplace; and another, a marble bathroom.

Bill and Peg supply guests with badminton and volleyball apparatus, hibachis and charcoal, coin-operated laundry facilities, and beach tags (for a small contribution). No meals are served, but shopping is nearby and each apartment has a kitchen.

Accommodations: 7 apartments with private bath. *Smoking:* Reluctantly permitted. *Children:* Permitted. *Pets:* Permitted if approved in advance. *Driving Instructions:* The Dormer House is in the middle of Cape May, two blocks from the fire station and the post office.

The Queen Victoria

102 Ocean Street, Cape May, NJ 08204. (609) 884-8702.
Hosts: Dane and Joan Wells.

The Wellses recently restored this large 1881 Victorian structure to its original appearance. The Sherwin-Williams Company has pointed to the house as perhaps the best example of color placement in Cape May. Joan used to be the executive director of the Victorian Society in America, and her fascination with Victoriana manifests itself throughout the house.

The bedrooms are furnished with authentic Victorian pieces, mostly of walnut, wicker, oak, and pine, along with fresh flowers and colorful quilts. The parlor, which features a huge fireplace, and the dining room are furnished with the Wellses' personal collection of Mission furniture. William Morris wallpapers, reproduced by hand-printing, cover the walls. The wallpaper in the dining room was designed for Queen Victoria, and Morris incorporated into the design the queen's initials and the imperial crown.

For guests who feel like exploring the town of Cape May or observing the ocean from a moving perspective, bicycles—one of them even built for two—are available. Farm eggs and cream, fresh fruit, homemade breads, and imported coffees and teas constitute the Wellses' complimentary breakfast.

Accommodations: 13 rooms, 5 with private bath. *Smoking:* Permitted in the parlor only. *Children:* Not permitted. *Pets:* Not permitted. *Breakfast:* Included. *Driving Instructions:* Take the Garden State Parkway to its end; continue straight on Route 109, which becomes Lafayette Street; in town, turn left at the second stoplight, Ocean Street, and proceed three blocks.

Cape May **NEW JERSEY**

The 7th Sister Guesthouse

10 Jackson Street, Cape May, NJ 08204. (609) 884-2280.
Hosts: Bob and JoAnne Myers.

Listed in the National Register of Historic Places, The 7th Sister is an 1888 Victorian Renaissance Revival structure with an imposing circular central staircase. The house, scarcely a hundred feet from the ocean, has a living room and several guest rooms that overlook the Atlantic.

The furnishings are 85 percent original, and to the original decor Bob and JoAnne have added a wicker collection of more than fifty pieces, a profusion of plants, and many of JoAnne's paintings. The parlor has its original coal-grate fireplace, and a sun porch faces the ocean. The side yard is taken up by a lawn and flowers.

Whether you're a history buff or love the outdoors, there's plenty to do in Cape May—swimming, sailing, canoeing, tennis, and antiquing are all major pastimes here.

Accommodations: 6 rooms with shared bath. *Smoking:* Permitted. *Children:* Over 7 permitted. *Pets:* Not permitted. *Driving Instructions:* Take the Garden State Parkway to its end; continue on Lafayette Street until it comes to a *T*, then make a left.

The Woolverton Inn

Woolverton Road, Stockton, New Jersey. Mailing address: Box 233, R.D. 3, Stockton, NJ 08559. (609) 397-0802. *Hostess:* Deborah Clark.

Situated on 10 acres of grounds that include parts of a sheep pasture and a formal garden, which Whitney North Seymour planted, the Woolverton Inn is a three-story Victorian stone manor house with an Italianate mansard roof. The house was built in 1793 by John Prall, the owner of a local quarry for whom Prallville, which is what Stockton used to be called, was named. There are porches on the first and second floors of the building.

Deborah Clark, who used to raise Siberian tigers for the Chrysler Marine Corporation, furnished the Woolverton Inn entirely with antiques. The living room has a fireplace with a wooden fanned mantel, an antique baby-grand piano, a 1930s French reproduction Louis XV chair upholstered with needlepoint, an Oriental rug in shades of blue and red, and etchings and drawings on the walls. The room faces directly south.

One guest room is a suite with three exposures, a king-size bed, and walls lined with bookcases, which contain some rare books. Each guest room features something different: There are a canopied bed with a matching cover and dust ruffle, a pair of 6-foot-tall four-poster, an Empire rocker, oriental rugs.

Deborah serves a Continental breakfast that includes fresh fruit, juices, and croissants and fancy breads.

Accommodations: 9 rooms with shared bath. *Smoking:* Permitted. *Children:* Not permitted. *Pets:* Permitted. *Breakfast:* Included. *Driving Instructions:* Take Route 29 north to Stockton, and then Route 533 for ¼ mile; turn left on Woolverton Road.

Bear Mountain Guest Ranch

P.O. Box 1163, Silver City, NM 88062. (505) 538-2538. *Hostess:* Myra B. McCormick.

Someone characterized Myra McCormick as a woman likely to have flapjacks in one hand and binoculars in the other. She is an active and erudite ornithologist and botanist. Hummingbirds sip nectar at her window feeders, and she has established a national reputation as a Wildplant Seekers Guide.

At an elevation of 6,250 feet, Myra's rambling hacienda features seven guest rooms with private baths; a four-bedroom house; a one-bedroom house; and a cottage. All guest rooms have porches with southern exposures.

Myra serves complimentary breakfast, lunch, and dinner and will prepare sack lunches for anyone who feels like exploring the countryside. Bear Mountain Guest Ranch is close to such natural wonders as hot springs and the Gila National Forest.

Accommodations: 7 rooms with private baths, 3 guest houses. *Smoking:* Permitted. *Children:* Permitted. *Pets:* Dogs on a leash permitted. *Breakfast, lunch, and dinner:* Included. *Driving Instructions:* From Silver City take Route I-80 toward Glenwood; turn right on Alabama Street, then turn left on the dirt road just beyond the cattle guard.

The Antique Mews

73 Main Street, Cold Spring, NY 10516. (914) 265-3727.
Host: Jack Kelly.

The Antique Mews is a four-story brick Federal structure that has been, over the years, a warehouse, an insurance company's offices, and a girls' finishing school. Today it's a combination antique shop and guest house.

Host Jack Kelly told me there's no knowing what kind of furnishings the front room and living room are likely to have at any given time, because antiques move in and out of his house like chess pieces. During my last visit, the living room contained an 1860s Third Empire gilded alcove bed, an early-American desk, and a Wedgwood music cabinet. An Oriental rug covers part of the living-room floor, and an antique American carpet of Chinese design covers another part of it.

One of the guest rooms is done in Art Deco and features an overstuffed sofa upholstered in a wine-colored velvet, chevron-design fabric curtains, and an armoire and coffee table that Jack designed himself. The other guest room, which has a working fireplace, sports walls covered in a Paisley fabric and is furnished in wicker.

Jack serves his guests a full breakfast, which consists of some sort of hot bread (such as popovers or biscuits), juice, melon, eggs or French toast, and bacon or sausage.

Accommodations: 2 rooms with private bath. *Smoking:* Permitted. *Children:* Permitted. *Pets:* Not permitted. *Breakfast:* Included. *Driving Instructions:* The Antique Mews is in the center of Cold Spring.

Cold Spring **NEW YORK**

One Market Street

1 Market Street, Cold Spring, NY 10516. (914) 265-3912.

Hosts: Philip and Esther Baumgarten.

Philip and Esther have a *circa*-1830 Federal-style house with a large yard shaded by mature trees. The house is one block from the Hudson River. Guests are welcome from March 15 through Christmas.

The guest suite has a small sitting room, a convertible couch, air conditioning, and a fully equipped kitchen, which is stocked with coffee and other morning essentials. The bedroom features a bed with a bamboo headboard, an old rocker and an old wicker chair, a 1930s radio that still works, and a grass rug on the floor. The walls are papered in a light and dark beige paper with a jungle-leaf pattern worked into it, and two large windows, with bamboo curtains, overlook a picturesque street. Each morning Philip and Esther bring their guests a newspaper, fresh buns, and fresh orange juice.

Accommodations: 1 suite with private bath. *Smoking:* Permitted. *Children:* Permitted. *Pets:* Not permitted. *Breakfast:* Included. *Driving Instructions:* The house is in the center of Cold Spring.

Rosewood Inn

134 East First Street, Corning, NY 14830. (607) 962-3253. *Hosts:* Dick and Winnie Peer.

The trees surrounding it date back only to 1880 or so, but the Rosewood Inn itself was built in 1860. Architecturally it is something of a hybrid, with elements of both Victorian and English Tudor design.

The house is a couple of short blocks from Corning's restored Market Street; a quick stroll across Centerway Bridge brings you to the Corning Glass Museum, which isn't made of glass but certainly houses a fascinating collection of it. Outdoor people will marvel at the beauty of New York's Finger Lakes region; indoor people will appreciate the area's many wineries, which feature free tastings and tours.

Winnie and Dick serve a complimentary breakfast, which includes homemade muffins and their special rosewood butter, in their paneled dining room.

Accommodations: 5 rooms, 3 with private bath. *Smoking:* Permitted. *Children:* Permitted. *Pets:* Permitted if well behaved. *Breakfast:* Included. *Driving Instructions:* One block south of Route 17, on East First Street.

The Golden Eagle Inn

Garrison's Landing, NY 10524. (914) 424-3067. *Hosts:* George and Stephanie Templeton.

Something of an architectural hybrid, a rectilinear Colonial of sorts with a slight Georgian feeling, the Golden Eagle is an 1848 brick building with eight square columns, four on a floor, supporting a roofed porch and second-floor veranda. The lawn extends from the front porch to the Hudson River, which flows by with a kind of lazy majesty. You can participate in the river's flow by watching it from your room or the veranda; or, if you wish, George and Stephanie will lend you a canoe and instruct you in its use.

Parts of the movie *Hello Dolly* were filmed on location at the Golden Eagle, which is decorated with a combination of genuine antiques and period reproductions. George and Stephanie used to be designers, and George's paintings, mostly of yachts, hang in the inn.

"We try to treat each of our guests as a houseguest and not just another body," says George. He and Stephanie especially enjoy sharing cocktails or wine with their guests before dinner. The Templetons serve a full complimentary breakfast, which guests can take in their room or on the veranda. Served with china and silver, it usually consists of freshly ground and brewed coffee, fresh fruit, warm croissants, and a selection of jams.

Accommodations: 6 rooms, 4 with private bath. *Smoking:* Permitted (cigars outdoors only). *Children:* Not Permitted. *Pets:* Not permitted. *Breakfast:* Included. *Driving Instructions:* Take Route 403 to Route 12; follow route 12 to its end and cross a small bridge; turn left and proceed 100 feet.

The Cobblestones

R.D. 2, Geneva, NY 14456. (315) 789-1896. *Hosts:* Mr. and Mrs. Lawrence Gracey.

Constructed of sandstone blocks, lake-washed and sorted according to size and color, The Cobblestones is an 1848 Greek Revival building. Four huge columns with Gothic capitols support the overhanging triangular pediment. Two smaller structures attached to the main house on either side also have columns holding up overhanging structures—in both cases, gabled roofs. Grounds comprise an acre of well-trimmed lawns with hedges and bushes and plenty of large shade trees.

Guest rooms are furnished primarily with antiques and period reproductions. The upstairs bedrooms still have their original old latches, and Oriental rugs appear all over the house.

Geneva is in one of New York State's lovelier areas, a lake region very active in agriculture. The New York State Agricultural Experiment Station, a branch of Cornell University, is close by, as are the Finger Lakes and their many facilities for fishing, boating, and swimming.

Accommodations: 3 rooms with shared bath. *Smoking:* Permitted. *Children:* Permitted. *Pets:* Permitted if well behaved. *Driving Instructions:* Take the New York State Thruway to exit 42 or exit 44 and continue into Geneva; then take Routes 5, 7, and 20 west for 3.5 miles.

Bridgehampton. A rock-bordered walkway leads to this ultramodern structure, which opens onto a wooded area that almost entirely surrounds it. The house features an observation deck—which overlooks the water—and a living room with modern furniture and a brick fireplace. *Represented by:* Lodgings Plus Bed & Breakfast, #4, (516) 324-6740 or (212) 858-9589. $60–$70.

Bridgehampton. A steep driveway leads to the hilltop where this secluded contemporary home is situated. The house is almost entirely surrounded by woods, but the grounds include a beautifully landscaped garden. The house, furnished with contemporary pieces, features a fireplace and a large deck that overlooks the garden. *Represented by:* Lodgings Plus Bed & Breakfast, #5, (516) 324-6740 or (212) 858-9589. $60–$70.

East Hampton. Encircled by trees, this contemporary house has a large deck wrapping around three sides of the second floor. The living room, which features a fireplace and modern furnishings, is on the second floor, which has a spiral staircase leading up to it. The house is a short walk from Gardiner's Bay. *Represented by:* Lodgings Plus Bed & Breakfast, #8, (516) 324-6740 or (212) 858-9589. $65–$75.

East Hampton. Directly on the beach, this isolated modern house features two decks, both of which offer spectacular views—there's a harbor off to the right and cliffs to the left (straight out there's only water). The living room has a Franklin stove, a Haitian cotton couch and rug, and a great deal of glass. *Represented by:* Lodgings Plus Bed & Breakfast, #9, (516) 324-6740 or (212) 858-9589. $75–$85.

East Hampton. This large cedar-shingled farmhouse near Gardiner's Bay has two fireplaces—one in the kitchen and the other in the living room. Simply furnished, the house is surrounded by grounds well planted with flowers. *Represented by:* Lodgings Plus Bed & Breakfast, #10, (516) 324-6740 or (212) 858-9589. $40–$50.

East Hampton. Several of the guest rooms here have private baths and working fireplaces. The house is furnished with a mixture of antique and contemporary pieces, and the guest rooms are similarly decorated. Wood-burning stoves seem to show up all over the place. The house is convenient to just about every-

Bridgehampton (*Lodgings Plus* #4)

Bridgehampton (*Lodgings Plus* #5)

thing in East Hampton, and the hosts have bicycles that guests may use. *Represented by:* Lodgings Plus Bed & Breakfast, # 11, (516) 324-6740 or (212) 858-9589. $50–$70.

East Hampton. Built of rough-hewn cedar, this modern house in a quiet wooded area is furnished with contemporary pieces. It has an open layout and features a deck that overlooks the woods. *Represented by:* Lodgings Plus Bed & Breakfast, #12, (516) 324-6740 or (212) 858-9589. $55–$65.

East Hampton. Hosted by a landscape architect, this house is directly on the beach. A wraparound deck and plenty of glass exposures take advantage of the house's spectacular views of Gardiner's Bay. The house has a Franklin stove and a large loft bedroom with a glass wall that overlooks the bay. *Represented by:* Lodgings Plus Bed & Breakfast, # 13, (516) 324-6740 or (212) 858-9589. $65–$75.

East Hampton. Surrounded by pine trees on a piece of land bordered by a rail fence, this guest house is only half a block from the beach. Hosted by a retired colonel, it features a patio with a flowering arbor. The host welcomes guests with a complimentary cocktail. *Represented by:* Lodgings Plus Bed & Breakfast, # 14, (516) 324-6740 or (212) 858-9589. $70.

Sag Harbor. Simply but comfortably furnished, this guest house is only a block from the beach. A quiet room with a semi-private bath is available for guests. *Represented by:* Lodgings Plus Bed & Breakfast, # 6, (516) 324-6740 or (212) 858-9589. $25.

Sag Harbor. Very close to Long Wharf, this Victorian home features a fireplace, a large backyard, and a deck. A short walk will take you into Sag Harbor, which is full of restaurants and other attractions, or to the beach. *Represented by:* Lodgings Plus Bed & Breakfast, # 7, (516) 324-6740 or (212) 858-9589. $30–$40.

Southampton. This typically New England-style cedar-shingled house on a tree-lined street is surrounded by large trees and a rail fence. The house has a large backyard, a comfortably furnished living room, and a convenient location—you can walk to Southampton Village, where there are plenty of fine shops and restaurants. *Represented by:* Lodgings Plus Bed & Breakfast, # 1, (516) 324-6740 or (212) 858-9589. $45–$55.

Southampton. Furnished with an eclectic mixture of antique

East Hampton (*Lodgings Plus* #9)

East Hampton (*Lodgings Plus* #10)

East Hampton (*Lodgings Plus* #13)

and contemporary pieces, this large late-nineteenth-century Victorian house features a living room with a brick fireplace, an Oriental rug, and many overstuffed chairs and couches. The hosts have a large collection of bric-a-brac, and the grounds feature a clay tennis court. Southampton Village is a short walk away. *Represented by:* Lodgings Plus Bed & Breakfast, # 2, (516) 324-6740 or (212) 858-9589. $60–$75.

Southampton. A contemporary home with hills behind it, this guest house has a large deck that overlooks a lake. The house is furnished simply but comfortably, and the guest room has a private bath. *Represented by:* Lodgings Plus Bed & Breakfast, #3, (516) 324-6740 or (212) 858-9589. $35.

East Hampton (*Lodgings Plus* #11)

House on the Hill

Box 86, High Falls, NY 12440. (914) 687-9627. *Hosts:* Shelly and Sharon Glassman.

Surrounded by locust, maple, evergreen, ash, and hickory trees, this eyebrowed Colonial structure was built in 1825. In 1856, a hand-forged iron fence appeared along the front lawn's perimeter; sometime after that, a colonial-style porch was added to the house. The property also contains a two-story wood-pegged barn, a smokehouse constructed of pink bricks, and a two-sided outhouse. The grounds feature thickly wooded areas and a pond.

Of the six guest rooms, one has a private bath and the other five share two baths. Every bed in the house is covered with a handmade quilt, and each guest room is furnished in Colonial style and comes with a bowl of fruit and freshly cut flowers.

The House on the Hill is minutes away from Lake Mohawk, New Paltz, Harley (famous for their many restored stone houses), and historic Kingston, which maintains a symphony orchestra.

Shelly and Sharon serve a full complimentary breakfast. When it's cold out, guests take it in the keeping room, which has the house's original fireplace and irons. Some guests prefer to eat breakfast on the glassed-in porch that faces the pond; others prefer it outdoors under the evergreens.

Accommodations: 6 rooms, 1 with private bath. *Smoking:* Permitted in the sitting room. *Children:* Permitted. *Pets:* Sometimes permitted; check first. *Breakfast:* Included. *Driving Instructions:* Take the New York State Thruway to exit 18 (New Paltz); take Route 299 West to the center of town; make a right onto Route 32 North; take Route 213 West into High Falls.

The Stagecoach Inn

Old Military Road, Lake Placid, NY 12946. (518) 523-9474. *Hosts:* Sherry and Pete Moreau.

The Stagecoach Inn was once a tavern where "people held elections, gathered for sport and horse trading, drank hard cider and sometimes liquids of a more stimulating character." The 1830 farmhouse was also once a post office and a sanctuary for one of Brigham Young's fleeing wives. The building was once owned by the man who invented the Dewey Decimal System (Melvil Dewey), and later by a president of Syracuse University.

Today the building is owned by Sherry and Peter Moreau, who have restored it—and have captured something of its more stimulating character. The building is in almost original condition. The Common Room, where guests tend to recount the events of their lives, has two fireplaces, one with a flintlock rifle hanging above it, and a birch log balcony spanning the length of the room. Some guest rooms feature brass beds or fireplaces or furniture original to the house.

Accommodations: 7 rooms, 3 with private bath. *Smoking:* Permitted. *Children:* Permitted. *Pets:* Permitted. *Breakfast:* Included. *Driving Instructions:* Take Route 86 or Route 73 to Old Military Road.

Roosevelt Island. This room, in the duplex apartment of a schoolteacher, has twin beds and shares a bath. It is on Roosevelt Island, a small and luxuriously developed island in the East River between the boroughs of Manhattan and Queens. Access to Manhattan, which is approximately 150 yards away, is either by car or, for those who enjoy convenience or beauty, via a monorail tramway that glides over the East River and, in ninety seconds or so, deposits you on Fifty-ninth Street and Second Avenue—one block from Bloomingdale's. *Represented by:* the B & B Group, (212) 838-7015. $35–$50.

The East 70s. This double room with a private bath, in the decorator-furnished home of a New York businesswoman, is in a luxurious building with a doorman and an elevator operator. From June through September you can, for a nominal fee, use the building's swimming pool. *Represented by:* the B & B Group, (212) 838-7015. $35–$55.

Near Lincoln Center. An assistant to the Dean of New York University, your hostess here offers a single and a double room, both with shared baths. The building, five minutes from Lincoln Center, is the residence of many prominent theater, television, and art-world people. *Represented by:* the B & B Group, (212) 838-7015. $30–$50.

The Fort Greene Historic Section. This guest accommodation is in a nineteenth-century brownstone that has leather wall coverings here and there. Your hosts serve a full breakfast, and their guest room, furnished with antiques, includes a sitting room. *Represented by:* Urban Ventures # 304, (212) MO 2-1234. $27.

The West 90s. You can sun yourself on the balcony of this nineteenth-floor apartment if you like; but even if you came to New York for something other than the sun, this accommodation has a beautiful view of New York and Central Park. The guest room, a double, has a canopy bed. "Of course use the kitchen." *Represented by:* Urban Ventures # 16, (212) MO 2-1234. $34–$42.

Featured in "House Beautiful." Many national magazines—*Redbook, New York, House Beautiful,* etc.—ran features on this apartment and, in separate articles, the quilts for which its owner is famous. You can rent the entire apartment or a single room. On West Eighty-second Street. *Represented by:* Urban Ventures # 102, (212) MO 2-1234. $48–$62.

East Seventy-eighth Street. This accommodation, which has a bathroom and a kitchen behind a hardly noticeable partition, has a working fireplace. The beds here are *futons*—a kind of Japanese sleeping quilt that many are replacing their current mattresses with. Near Central Park. *Represented by:* Urban Ventures Apt. 20, (212) MO 2-1234. $60.

Fifty-fifth off Fifth. A guest house that's convenient if you like to shop, or eat well, or visit the Museum of Modern Art and other Fifth Avenue attractions. Your hostess has decorated her home with the many handicrafts she brought from her native Hungary. *Represented by:* Urban Ventures # 31, (212) MO 2-1234. $36; $420 monthly.

East Eighty-fourth. This one-bedroom apartment, half a block from the Central Park Reservoir, is in an 1892 mansion convenient to the Metropolitan Museum of Art, the Madison Avenue boutiques, and the Guggenheim Museum. *Represented by:* Urban Ventures Apt. 24, (212) MO 2-1234. $66–$100.

Near Lincoln Center. "The highlight [of my trip] was the owner, who offered me a soft drink when I arrived—and was very friendly. On both mornings she brought coffee and toast to my room and even remembered I like to drink lots of ice water."—*The Travelbug.* This accommodation on the nineteenth floor of a high-rise is ten minutes from Lincoln Center. *Represented by:* Urban Ventures #105, (212) MO 2-1234. $35–$44.

East Sixty-Fifth. Your host, who has traveled the world taking photographs for *National Geographic,* offers guests a large bedroom with two exposures. This accommodation requires that you walk up five flights of steps; but the stairs, if it's any relief, are beautifully polished. *Represented by:* Urban Ventures #27, (212) MO 2-1234. $32–$38.

Park West Village. On Central Park West in the 90s, this newly decorated and furnished apartment is the home of a doctor and his sister. They offer a large double room with a private bath. This luxury elevator building—minutes from Central Park, the Museum of Natural History, and the Hayden Planetarium—has a security patrol and a security entrance. *Represented by:* the B & B Group, (212) 838-7015. $35–$50.

New York City (*Urban Ventures* #109)

New York City (*Urban Ventures* #410)

The East 50s. A restaurant-owner-turned-salesman, your host offers an air-conditioned room with television, which shares a bath. The building features an elevator and substantial security. *Represented by:* the B & B Group, (212) 838-7015. $35–$55.

The Upper West Side. A very savvy woman (she speaks Danish, English, and Hebrew), your hostess here offers a double-bedded room. A piano in the living room testifies to her interest in music. The location is convenient to Central Park. *Represented by:* the B & B Group, (212) 838-7015. $30–$50.

The West 90s. Your host is a stage and television actor who offers two rooms—one double with air conditioning and a ceiling fan, one single. Both share a bath. *Represented by:* the B & B Group, (212) 838-7015. $30–$50.

The Financial District. A double bedroom with a private bath in the downstairs section of a duplex apartment, which is actually a converted loft. A captain's ladder or a conventional staircase lead to a Jacuzzi. Your hosts, a pediatrics nurse and a computer salesman, are skiing and white-water enthusiasts. In the City Hall area, this accommodation is a short walk from Soho and Greenwich Village. *Represented by:* the B & B Group, (212) 838-7015. $30–$45.

Featured in "Redbook." Your hostess, who has a degree in education, arranges the curriculum for a New York City high school, operates a catering service, and conducts cooking classes. Her home, recently featured in *Redbook,* is a two-story brownstone in the West 80s. The house contains such niceties as wainscoting and cherry-wood paneling. Her upstairs living room can be used as a sitting room and bedroom. Share bath. *Represented by:* The B & B Group, (212) 838-7015. $35–$55.

The West 40s. A teacher of gifted children at New York University offers guests a clean, simple room that happens to be in the middle of the theater district. This accommodation is right across the street from Manhattan Plaza. *Represented by:* the B & B Group, (212) 838-7015. $25–$45.

Near Lincoln Center. Your hostess is a retired decorator who offers to guests a double bedroom decorated in Chinese motifs. The formal living room seats twelve. Five minutes from Lincoln center, Central Park, and most Upper West Side attractions. Television. *Represented by:* the B & B Group, (212) 838-7015. $35–$55.

The East 70s. Your hostess is a medical secretary who is fluent in Spanish. Portuguese, and Italian. She and her husband have a garden apartment, and the double bedroom they offer guests comes with a refrigerator, a television set, and a pinball machine. Share bath. *Represented by:* the B & B Group, (212) 838-7015. $30–$55.

Near the Museum of Natural History. Your hostess, a free-lance writer fluent in Spanish, offers a double bedroom with a private bath. Occasionally she has two bedrooms available (check in advance). This high-rise elevator building in the West 70s is within walking distance of Lincoln Center, the Hayden Planetarium, and the Museum of Natural History. *Represented by:* the B & B Group, (212) 838-7015. $30–$50.

View of Park. This guest room has a commanding view of a church spire, Central Park, and myriad New York City skyscrapers. Your host, an artist, responded: "Use the kitchen? Of course. Front room too—I'm so rarely home." *Represented by:* Urban Ventures #117, (212) MO 2-1234. $50.

Next to the Dakota. On West Seventy-third street, this accommodation, whose hosts are both in the theater, features a superb collection of Eastern and Western decorative art pieces. Walk to Lincoln Center or Central Park. *Represented by:* Urban Ventures #115, (212) MO 2-1234. $48–$52.

East Thirtieth. The building is a pre-Civil War brownstone in whose formal dining room, downstairs, breakfast is served. This accommodation is in a great location for shoppers, restaurant seekers and those who prefer the quieter parts of Manhattan. *Represented by:* Urban Ventures #410, (212) MO 2-1234. $58.

The Theater District. Your hostess, a jewelry maker and importer of rare items, comes from Curaçao. She offers guests a studio apartment with a kitchen and private bath. The location on West Forty-sixth Street is about as close as you can get to the Broadway theaters and Restaurant Row. *Represented by:* the B & B Group, (212) 838-7015. $35–$50.

The West 80s. Your host, a Ph. D. student at Columbia and a free-lance writer, offers guests a simple double room with a shared bath. This accommodation is five minutes from Lincoln Center and a short walk from Central Park. *Represented by:* the B & B Group, (212) 838-7015. $25–$40.

West 57th Street. This accommodation features a thirty-story-high panoramic view of New York City. The views are even better from the roof, where there is a health club accessible to guests. *Represented by:* Urban Ventures # 306, (212) MO 2-1234. $40–$48.

Near Lincoln Center. This accommodation is in an elegant, television-monitored building. All guests are announced. Your host is an advertising executive. *Represented by:* Urban Ventures #109, (212) MO 2-1234. $44–$52.

Antiques. An architect and a small dog offer guests the master bedroom of an antique-filled apartment. Private bath. *Represented by:* Urban Ventures #203, (212) MO 2-1234. $52.

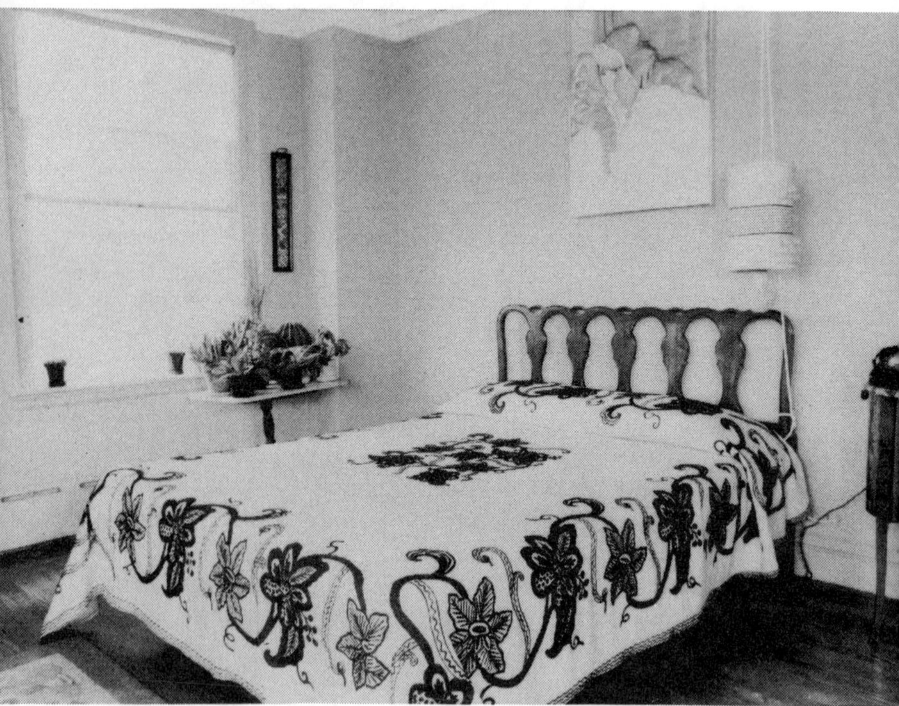

New York City (*Urban Ventures* #304)

Bed and Breakfast in Manhattan

139 West 87th Street, New York, NY 10024. (212) 496-6268. Hostesses: Judith Haber and Evelyne Jankowski.

Judith and Evelyne, who publish the *Chez des Amis Guide to French Host Families,* live in a century-old brownstone. On a quiet, tree-lined street, it features a private security service at night. The house has high ceilings and a lot of woodwork.

Each of the four guest rooms has a small refrigerator, a coffee maker, and a toaster and is stocked with the makings of a Continental breakfast. There are two baths and one powder room for guests. $35–$42.

The Tibbitts House

100 Columbia Turnpike, Rensselaer, NY 12144. (518) 472-1348. *Hosts:* Herb and Claire Rufleth.

This converted farmhouse dating from the 1850s, constructed of massive timbers fastened with square nails, is on the old Knox Trail (now Routes 9 and 20). The trail made it possible for General Knox and his troops, with a little help from a team of oxen, to drag a huge cannon, which the British would have preferred they had left at home, from Fort Ticonderoga to Boston.

The house is surrounded by trees, flower boxes with lilies and petunias, and manicured beds of iris and violets. Family owned and operated for the past fifty-five years, The Tibbitts House now features an 84-foot porch where Herb and Claire serve breakfast during the warmer months. The lounge, a converted keeping room, has exposed tree-trunk beams in the ceiling, a 12-foot oak and walnut church pew, a raised-hearth fireplace in the corner, and numerous hand-hooked scatter rugs.

For joggers, walkers, and bicyclists, there is a 45-mile path that runs along the west bank of the Hudson, 2 miles from the house.

Accommodations: 6 rooms, 1 with private bath. *Smoking:* Permitted. *Children:* Not permitted. *Pets:* Not permitted. *Driving Instructions:* On Routes 9 and 20 in Clinton Heights.

Candelite Inn

3 South Ferry (Route 114), Shelter Island, NY. *Mailing Address:* P.O. Box 644, Shelter Island, NY 11964. (516) 749-0788. *Hosts:* Joan and Harry Cass.

The Candelite Inn is a *circa*-1833 Victorian structure, with a wraparound porch supported by thin beams, and a great deal of delicate gingerbread trim. The grounds—lawns and hedges shaded by mature trees—include a small red barn in back of the house and several motel units in the side yard.

The six guest rooms in the main house share two baths; the four motel units have private baths and quickly transform into two-room family cottages. Guest rooms are immaculate and furnished simply with nice touches like maple bureaus and bedsteads. The rooms are carpeted, and the walls are covered with artificial wood paneling.

Joan and Harry serve a complimentary Continental breakfast each morning in their front room, and for other meals will recommend local restaurants to their guests.

Accommodations: 10 rooms, 4 with private bath. *Smoking:* Permitted. *Children:* Permitted. *Pets:* Not permitted. *Breakfast:* Included. *Driving Instructions:* The ferry to Shelter Island leaves you on Route 114.

The Bowditch House

166 North Ferry Road, Shelter Island, NY 11965. (516) 749-0075 or (516) 887-1898. *Hosts:* Jim and Nora Furey.

Originally part of a farm, the Bowditch House was built in 1854 and added to over the years. It currently has eighteen rooms. The house was built by Nathaniel Bowditch, who wrote *The American Practical Navigator,* and to be sure, Shelter Island is a place for practical navigators: A ten-minute ferry ride brings you to the island, which is just about traffic-free and has 57 miles of waterfront. Many guests leave their cars at home and use bicycles when they're on the island.

The guest rooms have fabric-covered walls and wide-board pine floors and are decorated individually with many antiques. One guest room has a carved oaken bed and dresser, a marble-topped night table, and an oaken reclining rocker. Another has a hand-painted bedroom set.

The living room, where Nora serves wine and tidbits in the afternoon, has a Victorian carved mahogany couch, maple floors, floor-to-ceiling windows that retain their original blown glass, and a child's desk and chair over in the corner. The room also has a nonworking fireplace and always has fresh flowers in it—as does every room in the house.

The Bowditch House is open weekends only from Memorial Day till Mid-June. From then on, it is open every day through Labor Day.

Accommodations: 9 rooms sharing 2 baths. *Smoking:* Permitted. *Children:* Under five not permitted. *Pets:* Not permitted. *Breakfast:* Included. *Driving Instructions:* The Shelter Island Ferry lets you off on North Ferry Road near the Bowditch House.

Bryson City. A short walk from the Deep Creek entrance to the Great Smoky Mountains National Park, Folkestone Lodge is an old farmhouse that has stone floors, claw-footed tubs, and stained-glass windows. Hosts Bob and Irene Dranich have antiques and Oriental rugs throughout the lodge, and breakfast is a special treat—the fare includes freshly baked breads, and the dining room has floor-to-ceiling windows overlooking mountains and woods. Open June through November. Route 1, West Deep Creek Road, Bryson City, NC 28713, (704) 488-2730. $22.50–$32.

Bryson City. In the family since 1895, Randolph House is a large multigabled structure with fieldstone pillars supporting an overhanging roof, which shades an area where guests relax amid large trees and well-tended lawns. Bill and Ruth Randolph Adams serve meals to guests as well as the public, although those not staying at the inn must make reservations. Six rooms are available, three with private baths. P.O. Box 816, Bryson City, NC 28713, (704) 488-3472. $80 for two, including breakfast and dinner.

Kill Devil Hills. Several of the guest rooms at Ye Olde Cherokee Inn have walls and ceilings of cypress. Two of the rooms face the ocean, and another two have views of the Wright Brothers Memorial, which is illuminated at night. The rooms are all carpeted and have air conditioning and cable television. Tom and Phyllis Combs don't serve breakfast, but guests are offered a cup of coffee to get them going in the morning. P.O. Box 315, Kill Devil Hills, NC 27948, (919) 441-6127. $15–$45.

Nags Head. A large Nags Head–style house with wraparound porches on the first and second floors, First Colony Inn has 400 feet of oceanfront property. Guests are invited to use the private beach, and to attend the watermelon festival that hosts Tim Shrewsbury and Wayne Melchor conduct each Wednesday. Half the rooms face the ocean, and all have private baths; efficiencies and cottages are also available. P.O. Box 938, Nags Head, NC 27959, (919) 441-7365. $34–$63.

Ocracoke. On the very shore of Silver Lake and 3 minutes from the ocean, Beach House has four rooms available: Two face the lake, and another has a view of the U.S. Coast Guard Station. The house has a front porch that overlooks the lake and Ocracoke Lighthouse. Hosts Tom and Carol Beach serve a full breakfast of homemade breads and jellies with bacon and eggs. P.O. Box 443, Ocracoke, NC 27960, (919) 928-6471. $27.

Cleveland Heights. Hosted by a physician and a teacher, this accommodation features a convertible couch and a private half bath. The hosts welcome extra guests willing to sleep in sleeping bags, and their location is convenient to all of Cleveland's attractions. *Represented by:* The International Spareroom, O-17, (714) 755-3194. $8.45–$16.90.

Quaker City. A nine-room house on a 285-acre farm, this guest house is hosted by people who serve homemade breads and homegrown vegetables. The location is convenient for hunting, fishing, swimming, boating, and golf. *Represented by:* The International Spareroom, O-16, (714) 755-3194. Rates on request.

Zanesfield. This guest house is a furnished trailer on a working farm that has 100 acres of woods and hills. Fishing, swimming, hayrides, and farm activities are available for guests to enjoy, and nearby there are castles and caverns to explore. *Represented by:* The International Spareroom, O-15, (714) 755-3194. Rates on request.

Akron **OHIO**

Portage House

601 Copley Road, Akron, OH 44320. (216) 535-9236.
Hosts: Harry and Jeanne Pinnick.

A large 1917 Tudor structure, the Portage House is on an acre that used to be part of the Perkins farm. The Perkinses were the founding family of Akron, and their original house as well as the stone wall surrounding it still stand. A plaque on the stone wall notes that this piece of land was, in 1785, the western boundary of the United States.

Harry and Jeanne Pinnick offer guests a variety of accommodations. There are three bedrooms with shared baths, a kitchenette apartment with a private bath, and a large bedroom with a fireplace and a private bath. Harry and Jeanne serve a complimentary Continental breakfast; for the truly hungry they will cook a full morning meal for a slight charge.

Accommodations: 5 rooms, 2 with private bath. *Smoking:* Permitted. *Children:* Permitted. *Pets:* Permitted. *Breakfast:* Included. *Driving Instructions:* Take Route I-77 to Route 162 (Copley Road), and proceed 2 miles east on Copley Road.

The Frederick Fitting House

72 Fitting Avenue, Bellville, OH 44813. (419) 886-4283.
Hosts: Rick and Jo Sowash.

This 1863 Victorian structure, with elaborate filigree and arched shutters on every window, was built by Frederick Fitting, a prominent Bellville citizen. Another prominent citizen, Johnny Appleseed, left his mark in the nearby forests. Jo and Rick honor his memory by serving apple butter with breakfast.

Rick is the executive director of Mansfield's historic Renaissance Theatre (whose classical and country-and-western performers often stay as guests in his home), a published novelist and an award-winning classical composer. Jo has degrees in English and registered nursing.

The living room is warmed by a large fireplace and has a library containing more than three thousand volumes. The house features 11-foot ceilings; a free-standing staircase of walnut, butternut, and oak; an elaborately hand-stenciled dining room; and a bathroom with Victorian fixtures—a claw-foot tub, a pedestal sink, and an Italian tile floor with matching wallpaper. The Sowashes serve a complimentary breakfast. As Rick puts it, "Our home is our hobby, and hosting guests is our joy."

Accommodations: 3 rooms with shared bath. *Smoking:* Not permitted. *Children:* Permitted. *Pets:* Permitted but not in the house (there is a large fenced-in yard). *Breakfast:* Included. *Driving Instructions:* Midway between Cleveland and Columbus, Bellville is 3 miles east of Route I-71 on Route 97. Enter the village on Route 97 and turn left at Fitting Avenue.

The Cider Mill

Second Street, P.O. Box 441, Zoar, OH 44697. *Hosts:* Ralph and Judy Kraus

The entire village of Zoar is listed in the National Register of Historic Places. The Cider Mill, a banked barn whose first and second floors both have a ground-floor entrance, was built in 1863. The first floor houses an antique and gift shop; the second floor is a Victorian living room; and the guest rooms and owners' quarters are on the third floor. Guests travel from one floor to the other by way of a spiral staircase.

All of the building's original beams have been exposed, as have the sandstone wall in the antique shop and the brick wall in the living room. The two guest rooms share a bath.

Ralph and Judy serve a full complimentary breakfast, permit children, and even arrange for baby-sitters. They permit pets, too, providing the visiting animals are compatible with the resident three dogs and a cat. Many attractions are nearby, including eight old buildings maintained by the Ohio Historical Society that are open to the public from April through October.

Accommodations: 2 rooms with shared bath. *Smoking:* Permitted. *Children:* Permitted. *Pets:* Permitted if compatible with resident animals. *Breakfast:* Included (gourmet meals provided at an additional charge). *Driving Instructions:* Located 3 miles east of Route I-77 and 15 miles south of Canton.

Arch Cape. Less than a block from the ocean and with an unobstructed view of it, this contemporary house is 6 miles from Cannon Beach, an artists' colony with many shops and a summer theater. You can see the ocean while breakfasting. *Represented by:* Northwest Bed & Breakfast, #302, (503) 246-8366 or 246-2383. $20–$28.

Bandon. You can see whales, sea lions, and fabulous sunsets from the large deck that wraps around the ocean side of this house, which is perched on a bluff about 40 feet above the ocean, to which you can easily walk. The hosts, whose hobbies include wine-making and rock-polishing, welcome contract-bridge players. *Represented by:* Northwest Bed & Breakfast, #310, (503) 246-8366 or 246-2383. $20–$34.

Depoe Bay. Depoe Bay and the Pacific come into panoramic perspective when viewed from this home on a hillside. The hosts welcome women, couples, and families. *Represented by:* Northwest Bed & Breakfast, #305, (503) 246-8366 or 246-2383. $20–$34.

Dexter. A farm homestead 14 miles south of Eugene, this accommodation features a hot tub, which is on a deck that overlooks a meadow. The house has a pool table, which guests are invited to use. A professional couple, the hosts enjoy organizing activities. *Represented by:* Northwest Bed & Breakfast, #432, (503) 246-8366 or 246-2383. $18–$40.

Gleneden Beach. An ideal location from which to watch whales, this home is on the oceanfront, near a beach, and you needn't go far for golf or indoor tennis. Guests are invited to use the whirlpool tub. *Represented by:* Northwest Bed & Breakfast, #304, (503) 246-8366 or 246-2383. $20–$24.

Grants Pass. This house, which overlooks the Roque River, features a private dock from which guests can go fishing or boating. The hosts, who speak Spanish as well as English, come from very different backgrounds—a test pilot and a businesswoman. *Represented by:* Northwest Bed & Breakfast, #490, (503) 246-8366 or 246-2383. $20–$34.

Gresham. Twenty miles east of Portland, this contemporary home has a view of the Sandy River. The house has a veranda, which enables guests to take in views of the wooded areas surrounding the house. Outdoor people, the hosts have interests that range from mushroom-hunting to carving totem poles. *Represented by:* Northwest Bed & Breakfast, #377, (503) 246-8366 or 246-2383. $14–$26.

Hillsdale. When the weather's good, the hosts serve breakfast by their pool, which is surrounded by a garden. Literature and art—as well as swimming, of course—appeal to the hosts, a business-and-professional couple. *Represented by:* Northwest Bed & Breakfast, #362, (503) 246-8366 or 246-2383. $18–$34.

Lincoln City. Twelve blocks from the ocean and overlooking Devils Lake, this home features a pool and a Ping-Pong table, both of which guests are invited to use. *Represented by:* Northwest Bed & Breakfast, #303, (503) 246-8366 or 246-2383. $20.

Molalla. With 5 acres of land where guests are invited to fish, this accommodation is 27 miles from Portland. The hosts, who are interested in genealogy, serve breakfast on their enclosed patio. Guests are invited to picnic by the creek, which has a waterfall. *Represented by:* Northwest Bed & Breakfast, #402, (503) 246-8366 or 246-2383. $20–$30.

Newport. A retired professor and his wife welcome guests to their antique-furnished home, which overlooks the ocean and Yaquina Head. The house, near a golf course, features a fireplace. The hosts' hobbies are working in stained glass and baking. *Represented by:* Northwest Bed & Breakfast, #307, (503) 246-8366 or 246-2383. $16–$20.

Portland. This 1890 Victorian house in the hills that overlook Portland features a shaded deck with woods all around. The hosts are legal professionals—an attorney and a counselor. *Represented by:* Northwest Bed & Breakfast, #350, (503) 246-8366 or 246-2383. $18–$30.

Portland. The host of this accommodation in Southwestern Portland is a poet, and a dog and a cat are also in residence. The house, fifteen minutes from downtown Portland, is in a peaceful neighborhood and has a garden. *Represented by:* Northwest Bed & Breakfast, #367, (503) 246-8366 or 246-2383. $15–$22.

Portland. This downtown accommodation, which has an outdoor pool and sun decks, is in a condominium. Music and theater appeal to the host, whose condominium is within walking distance of many of Portland's cultural attractions. *Repre-*

sented by: Northwest Bed & Breakfast, #368, (503) 246-8366 or 246-2383. $18.50–$26.00.

Redmond. This house, built and designed by the owner, features a deck that faces nearby mountains, offering spectacular views of Black Butte and the Cascades. *Represented by:* Northwest Bed & Breakfast, #453, (503) 246-8366 or 246-2383. $20–$30.

West Lind. Fifteen miles south of Portland, this ranch-style house has choice views of the confluence of the Clackamas and Willamette rivers and of Mount Hood and Mount St. Helens. The hosts—a writer–chemical engineer and a legal assistant—are fond of guiding their guests around Portland. *Represented by:* Northwest Bed & Breakfast, #381, (503) 246-8366 or 246-2383. $14.

Spring House

Muddy Creek Forks, Airville, PA 17302. (717) 927-6906.
Hostess: Ray Constance Hearne.

Ray Hearne prefers the aesthetic to the practical, which explains (at least partially) why she undertook to restore singlehandedly a 1798 stone house that one realtor called a "stone ruin," why she does all her cooking on and heats her house exclusively with wood stoves, why she commissioned an artist to do stencil work on her walls, and why she lives in a town whose population is 17.

All of the guest-room beds are covered with handmade quilts and coverlets. One room has a spool model bed and a wood stove. For those allergic to electric blankets, Ray offers a solution to cold sheets—she warms them with heated soapstones, which she leaves, safely wrapped, at the foot of your bed.

The house features floors of oak or pine, numerous Oriental rugs, some preserved 1840s stencil work, many original paintings, and whitewashed walls. Ray's complimentary breakfast is full—sausage, eggs, fruit, homemade muffins, coffee, and juice.

Accommodations: 3 rooms with shared baths. *Smoking:* Not permitted. *Children:* Permitted. *Pets:* Occasionally permitted. *Breakfast:* Included. *Driving Instructions:* Take Route 74 south to the village of Brogue, turn right at the post office, and go 5 miles to Muddy Creek Forks.

The Homestead

785 Baltimore Street, Gettysburg, PA 17325. (717) 334-2037. *Hosts:* Ruth S. Wisler and Marie V. Scott.

Located at the edge of Gettysburg Battlefield, the Homestead was built in 1869 as the annex to an orphanage. The story has it that after the Battle of Gettysburg someone found in the hand of a dead soldier a daguerreotype of that soldier's three children. This prompted the citizens of Gettysburg to build an orphanage, and when three years later the increasing numbers of orphans required another building to house them, the citizens erected the Homestead. The third floors of both buildings served as dormitories, the original building (a museum now) housed the dining room and kitchen, and the school was in the annex. The Homestead has on display reproductions of early photographs of the orphanage and its occupants. Shortly after its last director was dismissed for mistreating the children (there's a dungeon in the cellar where the children were punished) the orphanage closed and the buildings became private dwellings.

Today The Homestead is furnished with heirloom antiques, some dating from as far back as the early nineteenth century. Much of the furniture was brought here from Germany by hostess Ruth Wisler's grandparents. The living room has an antique drop-leaf table, an old Boston rocker, a set of Ruth's grandmother's ladder-back chairs, several electrified kerosine lamps (including two revitalized nickel Rayo lamps), a corner cupboard, an organ, and an antique dry sink. The guest rooms are simply but comfortably furnished.

Accommodations: 6 rooms with shared bath. *Smoking:* Permitted. *Children:* Permitted. *Pets:* Not permitted. *Driving Instructions:* The Homestead is on Route 97, near the National Cemetery.

Maple Lane Guest House

505 Paradise Lane, Paradise, PA 17562. (717) 687-7479.
Hosts: Edwin and Marion Rohrer.

In the heart of Pennsylvania Dutch country, the Maple Lane Guest House is part of a 250-acre working farm that has 180 head of cattle, a hundred or so of them milk cows. The farmland here consists of rolling valley meadows (you can see for 40 miles from above one of them) with patches of wooded areas. A stream winds through the property, and 2 acres of lawn and a few mature maple trees surround the main farmhouse, a modern Colonial-style home painted green and beige.

The living room has white walls trimmed in Williamsburg blue, a curved walnut Victorian sofa upholstered in a rose- and shell-colored tapestry fabric, an antique cherry smokestand end table, off-white carpeting, and an electric organ. Like the living room, the guest rooms are furnished primarily with antiques, and every bed in the house is covered with a handmade quilt. Marion, like many of her Amish neighbors, makes quilts by hand and does needlepoint.

Across from the new farmhouse is the old farmhouse, where Marion and Edwin's son now lives—an 1875 fieldstone structure built by a German immigrant.

The Maple Lane Guest House is close to any number of Pennsylvania Dutch–country attractions: A wax museum, the Pennsylvania Farm Museum, and the Robert Fulton House are all nearby. The farm itself is an attraction, especially around milking time, and guests are welcome to watch the doing of farm chores.

Accommodations: 4 rooms, 2 with private bath. *Smoking:* Permitted. *Children:* Permitted. *Pets:* Not permitted. *Driving Instructions:* From Strasburg, turn south on Route 896 and proceed for 1.5 miles. Look for the sign of the Timberline Lodge, which is on Paradise Lane.

Society Hill Town House. This three-story town house, on a quiet street in the middle of Philadelphia's Historic District, offers two guest rooms, both with air conditioning and television and sharing a bath. Decorated in Colonial style, the living room has sliding glass doors that overlook the patio. Your hostess, a businesswoman, knows the city and its surrounding areas well. Full complimentary breakfast. *Represented by:* Bed & Breakfast of Philadelphia, (215) 884-1084. $25–$30.

Lansdowne International. A mile and a half from the city line, thirty-five minutes by bus to the center of town, this accommodation is in a large house that contains a stone fireplace as wide as the room it's in. There's a grand piano in the living room (your hosts love classical music), and an eighteenth-century canopied bed in the guest room. For a mileage fee, your host, a member of the Scottish Historical Society, chauffeurs/guides international visitors. He welcomes cats and dogs, speaks German, and serves a full breakfast. *Represented by:* Bed & Breakfast of Philadelphia, (215) 884-1084. $15–$22.

Radnor Charm. Twenty-five minutes by train from central Philadelphia, this 107-year-old house offers two guest rooms, both with a television set and a private bath, as well as tile-faced fireplaces and large low-sill windows facing high tree-branches. Your hosts serve a full breakfast, either in their Colonial breakfast room or on their screened-in porch. *Represented by:* Bed & Breakfast of Philadelphia, (215) 884-1084. $25–$30.

Jarreton Farmhouse. This 150-year-old farmhouse, thirty-five minutes by train from the center of town, offers up to four guest rooms (sometimes the children visit). Wood stoves heat the sitting room, the family room, and one bedroom. The water is solar-heated. Excepting the three midweek days she works, your hostess serves a full breakfast—the rest of the time do-it-yourself ingredients are available. *Represented by:* Bed & Breakfast of Philadelphia, (215) 884-1084. $16–$23.

Strafford Village. A public relations/advertising manager and business/craftswoman are your hosts in this Colonial home seven minutes from Valley Forge National Historic Park. During the summers they serve breakfast in their lush garden, under a yellow umbrella. *Represented by:* Bed & Breakfast of Philadelphia, (215) 884-1084. $18–$24.

Valley Forge Apartment. Forty-five minutes from the center of Philadelphia, this apartment offers a balcony and an indoor/outdoor swimming pool. Your hostess teaches at a technical school and has a collection of San Blas Indian *molas* in her living room. *Represented by:* Bed & Breakfast of Philadelphia, (215) 884-1084. $15–$25.

Pineapple Hill—New Hope. The dining room here has a fireplace and 18-inch-thick walls. Guests are invited to use the pool, which is in the ruins of a stone barn. The guest rooms, most with sloping walls, have brass or spool beds and simple country furnishings. *Represented by:* Bed & Breakfast of Philadelphia, (215) 884-1084. $30.

West Chester Suite. A separate suite of rooms in a Colonial home slightly west of Philadelphia, this accommodation has a private entrance, a color television set with cable, and air conditioning. The guest suite is furnished after the style of the early 1920s—the 1980s are represented by an individually controlled thermostat. *Represented by:* Bed & Breakfast of Philadelphia, (215) 884-1084. $18–$26.

West Chester circa 1840. Forty-five minutes by bus from town, surrounded by old trees, this accommodation is in a "summer home" that sits on a curved knoll. There are high ceilings, tall windows, and a fireplace in the den. With a large corporation until recently, your host knows the area well, especially activities at the University of Pennsylvania. *Represented by:* Bed & Breakfast of Philadelphia, (215) 884-1084. $20–$28.

Wyndmoor Victorian. Keenly interested in the history and sociology of Philadelphia, and thirty minutes distant from it by commuter train, your hosts are involved in public service and medicine. Once in a while their college-age children liven up the house, which has a tree-shaded lawn and bicycles for those so inclined. *Represented by:* Bed & Breakfast of Philadelphia, (215) 884-1084. $22–$30.

Philadelphia **PENNSYLVANIA**

Society Hill Hotel

Third and Chestnut streets, Philadelphia, PA 19106. (215)925-1394. *Hosts:* David DeGraff and Judith Baird Campbell.

The Society Hill Hotel is an 1832 red-brick building across the street from the Federal Visitor's Center and Independence Historic National Park. The building is trimmed in Williamsburg red, except those parts of it that are made of marble, such as the front steps.

The guest rooms have pale gray walls and charcoal gray wall-to-wall carpeting, burgundy hand stenciling and crown moldings, and brass double beds. Historical prints and lithographs appear in all the rooms, which are furnished with a combination of antique and traditional furnishings. All of the guest rooms have private baths, some of which retain their antique brass fixtures, and each bath comes complete with a hair dryer and Eurobath soap. There are fresh flowers in every room.

Breakfast is served on a wicker tray decorated with fresh flowers and brought to your room at the time you request. The Society Hill Hotel has a bar-restaurant characterized by light woods, stained glass, and plenty of plants.

Accommodations: 12 rooms with private bath. *Smoking:* Permitted. *Children:* Permitted. *Pets:* Not permitted. *Breakfast:* Included. *Driving Instructions:* The hotel is in the heart of Philadelphia's Old City and Society Hill, directly across the street from the Federal Visitor's Center.

The Brinley

23 Brinley Street, Newport, RI 02840. (401) 849-7645.
Hosts: George and Christine Van Duinwyk.

George and Christine have an 1871 Victorian home, which was originally built by one Joseph Tews, a man who seems to have eluded history, albeit there's a nearby street named after him. Christine figures the layout of the building is such that it was probably designed to be a rooming house.

The guest rooms, which come with fresh flowers and turned-down beds with mints on their pillows, are furnished with Victorian antiques. Three of these rooms have nonworking fireplaces; some feature 9-foot-wide bay windows; all have matching bedspreads and curtains. The parlor has a Victorian curved, claw-footed couch covered in mauve fabric, side tables covered with lace, and a floral Sarouk rug.

George and Christine both have teaching backgrounds. Christine still teaches art in a nearby junior high school, and George, who previously taught design at the Rhode Island Institute of Design and at Kent State University, recently became president of the Quest Association of Newport County, an association of guest houses.

Accommodations: 10 rooms, 3 with private bath. *Smoking:* Permitted. *Children:* Under 10 not permitted. *Pets:* Not permitted. *Breakfast:* Included. *Driving Instructions:* The Brinley is near the center of Newport.

Dennis Guest House

59 Washington Street, Newport, RI 02840. (401) 846-1324.
Host: The Reverend Henry G. Turnbull.

Dennis House is a 1740 Colonial structure, with an elaborate pineapple-front doorway and a fabulous widow's walk (the only flat one in Newport). The house is also the rectory of Saint John's Episcopal Church.

Father Turnbull, who has been rector of Saint John's for more than twenty years, decided to turn the rectory into a guest house because the costs of maintaining the building were getting out of hand. "Now," Father Turnbull proudly says, "the rectory supports itself so well I've removed it from the parish budget."

Father Turnbull told me that his guest house is not religiously oriented. "It's nice to have a little break from solely religious matters," he said, "and meeting with as many people as I have has been an absolutely ecumenical experience."

In addition to being a rector, Father Turnbull is also something of an antiques collector. The guest rooms feature such items as Victorian reproduction stripe and print wallpapers, country antiques, kilimlike Yugoslavian rugs, and, in one room, a 9- by 12-foot blue-and-gray Oriental. Two of the guest rooms have working fireplaces.

The parlor, which Father Turnbull calls the hospitality center, features electrified wrought-iron wall sconces, a wall of exposed brick, built-in bookcases containing an extensive collection of books, and a view of Narragansett Bay and the Newport Bay Bridge.

Accommodations: 3 rooms with private bath. *Smoking:* Permitted. *Children:* Not permitted. *Pets:* Not permitted. *Breakfast:* Included. *Driving Instructions:* Dennis House is in the center of Newport, next to Saint John's Episcopal Church.

Bay Street Inn

601 Bay Street, Beaufort, SC 29902. (803) 524-7720. *Hosts:* David and Terry Murray.

Listed in the National Register of Historic Places, the Bay Street Inn is an 1852 mansion with six Ionic-over-Doric columns supporting two verandas. During the Civil War the house functioned as a Union officers' club and when things got worse, as a hospital.

Each guest room is furnished with antiques, which range from period French pieces to a grand old Carolina rice bed, and each has a fireplace and a sitting area. The public rooms feature fine plaster- and woodwork, high ceilings, and two fireplaces.

The Murrays include in their rates a great many complimentary extras—breakfast, the morning paper, a fruit basket, a decanter of sherry, evening chocolates, and bicycles. David and Terry serve breakfast on china, with crystal and sterling.

The house, whose grounds contain azalea, dogwood, and crepe myrtle, overlooks South Carolina's intercoastal waterway.

Accommodations: 5 rooms with private bath. *Smoking:* Permitted. *Children:* School-age children permitted. *Pets:* Not permitted. *Breakfast:* Included. *Driving Instructions:* From Savannah, take Route 17-A north; then take Route 120 into Beauport.

Barrett House (*Historic Charleston Bed & Breakfast*)

Jeffords House. An 1843 Greek Revival structure, Jeffords House features a wrought-iron gate that leads to a private patio. The patio, in turn, leads to a garden next to an old carriage house that now serves as the guest quarters. Both houses are furnished with a blend of antique and modern pieces. *Represented by:* Historic Charleston Bed & Breakfast, (803) 722-6606. $65–$90.

Barrett House. Built in 1875, Barrett House has a porch and a veranda that overlook its private garden, to which each of the three guest rooms has access. The house's original oven and kitchen fireplace are still there, as are the wide-board wooden floors. Each guest accommodation (all of them restored) has its own living room. *Represented by:* Historic Charleston Bed & Breakfast, (803) 722-6606. $60.

Jeffords House (*Historic Charleston Bed & Breakfast*)

Watkins-Thomas House. A *circa*-1720 structure, Watkins-Thomas House has a carriage house available for guests. This carriage house is listed in the National Register of Historic Places and features exposed-beam ceilings and a clay-tile roof. The grounds include a formal garden. *Represented by:* Historic Charleston Bed & Breakfast, (803) 722-6606. $60.

Chapman House. Chapman House, built in 1795, has two rooms for guests. A sunny third-floor garret room contains antique French twin beds, and a second-floor room has an antique four-poster. Breakfast is served on silver trays. *Represented by:* Historic Charleston Bed & Breakfast (803) 722-6606. $60.

Leopard's House. Furnished with a combination of antiques from Leopard's Shop and period reproductions, this 1890s structure is in the heart of Charleston's antique district. The guest quarters feature a private piazza where guests may take their breakfast. *Represented by:* Historic Charleston Bed & Breakfast, (803) 722-6606. $60.

Rice House. Rice House's guest quarters overlook Charleston's harbor. The house, built around 1812, has on its grounds a swimming pool that guests are invited to use. *Represented by:* Historic Charleston Bed & Breakfast, (803) 722-6606. $60.

Two Meeting Street Inn

2 Meeting Street at the Battery, Charleston, SC 29401. (803) 723-7322. *Hostess:* Lois Fender.

To prevent plaster from falling onto the food during earthquakes (the Charleston quake of 1886 having leveled the building previously occupying the same site), its builders specified that the dining room and foyer of this 1892 Queen Anne Victorian mansion have ceilings made of oak. Worried though they might have been about falling plaster, they didn't worry at all about breaking glass: The dining room has a 6-foot sunburst stained-glass window above a built-in china cabinet; and the living room, dining room, foyer, and staircase landing all have Tiffany stained-glass windows.

The building is surrounded on two sides by arched piazzas that face the Battery Park across the street. The columned bandstand in the park was presented to the city of Charleston by this inn's original owners, a family enamored of listening to concerts while sipping mint juleps on their piazza.

Five of the guest rooms have private baths, as well as seventeenth-century Dutch-tiled fireplaces. The furnishings throughout the house include such goodies as Persian and other Oriental rugs, old blue-and-white Canton china, brass chandeliers, carved oaken paneling, and easy chairs covered with needlepoint. The entire building is centrally air-conditioned and heated.

Accommodations: 9 rooms, 5 with private bath. *Smoking:* Permitted. *Children:* Under 6 not permitted. *Pets:* Not permitted. *Driving Instructions:* Take Route I-95 to Route I-26 East, and exit at its terminus onto Meeting Street.

Bristol. This guest house is on a knoll in the middle of a 52-acre tobacco farm. The guest room, furnished with antiques, overlooks the Holsten River and the surrounding mountains, and the grounds contain a swimming pool, which guests are invited to use. In a kitchen with a fireplace, the hosts serve a full Southern breakfast. *Represented by:* Hospitality Plus Bed & Breakfast, TN-103, (205) 259-1298. $20–$25.

Jonesboro. This accommodation is in a brick, Ranch-style home, a short walk from Historic Jonesboro. Guests are invited to relax in the yard, and the hosts serve a full country breakfast. Lifetime residents of the area, the hosts will point out places not listed in brochures or guidebooks. *Represented by:* Hospitality Plus Bed & Breakfast, TN-102, (205) 259-1298. $20–$25.

Jonesboro. A fine base for history buffs, this 1875 home is a few blocks from the Main Street of Historic Jonesboro, the oldest town in Tennessee. Fifteen of the homes in town are listed in the National Register of Historic Places, and the host is willing to take guests on a tour of them in his 1919 Model T depot hack. *Represented by:* Hospitality Plus Bed & Breakfast, TN-101, (205) 259-1298. $18–$23.

Near Centennial Park. Fifteen minutes from the airport and 3 minutes from "Music Row," this apartment couldn't be closer to Nashville's famous night spots. Centennial Park and Vanderbilt University are also close by. The hostess—who welcomes women, couples, or families with a small child—enjoys accompanying her guests on weekend tours around town. *Represented by:* Nashville Bed & Breakfast, A-0301, (615) 327-4546. $18–$32.

Foreign Visitors Only. This guest house, whose hosts are both lawyers, welcomes foreign visitors only. French, Spanish, Russian, and Thai guests will all find conversation available in this household, which features an outdoor swimming pool and a hot tub. *Represented by:* Nashville Bed & Breakfast, A-0501, (615) 327-4546. $23–$29.

Near "Music Row." Hosted by a young professional couple, this guest house is in a complex with a swimming pool. Two free tennis courts are a short walk down the street. Between them, the hosts speak French, German, and Spanish, as well as English. Close by are "Music Row" and downtown Nashville. *Represented by:* Nashville Bed & Breakfast, A-0503, (615) 327-4546. $21–$34.

Near Cumberland River. Twelve minutes from the airport, on 60 acres of undeveloped land, this guest house is close to the Cumberland River marinas and Cheatham Dam. The second-floor accommodation features a large balcony–sun deck. *Represented by:* Nashville Bed & Breakfast, A-0901, (615) 327-4546. $20–$61.

Near Vanderbilt University. Two and a half miles from downtown, this brick, Cape Cod–style house is hosted by a young pastoral counselor. Pets are welcome. Guests who stay a long time are invited to use the kitchen and the laundry facilities. *Represented by:* Nashville Bed & Breakfast, A-1204, (615) 327-4546. $20–$45.

Former Church. This building used to be a church, and what used to be a choir loft is now a guest room with a Jacuzzi. The Tennessee Historical Commission cited this home as a creative example of adaptive restoration. The hosts speak French and Spanish, as well as English, and their home is 15 minutes from downtown Nashville. *Represented by:* Nashville Bed & Breakfast,

A-2101, (615) 327-4546. $25–$84.

Doctor in the House. Fifteen minutes from downtown Nashville, this guest house is hosted by a young physician and his family. The guest quarters consist of two rooms, which can accommodate as many as five people. One of the rooms has a fireplace, electronic games, a patio, and a private entrance. French and German (as well as English) are spoken. *Represented by:* Nashville Bed & Breakfast, B-1701, (615) 327-4546. $20–$61.

Twenty Minutes From Opryland. This guest house features an accommodation with its own living room, bedroom, kitchen, and private entrance. Children are welcome. *Represented by:* Nashville Bed & Breakfast, C-7502, (615) 327-4546. $22–$69.

Mini-Farm. A mini-farm with horses, this home has guest quarters that are detached from the main house. The guest quarters have a bedroom, a small refrigerator, and a private bath. When they're home, the hosts allow guests to ride their horses. Opryland is only 20 minutes away. *Represented by:* Nashville Bed & Breakfast, D-2703, (615) 327-4546. $20–$45.

Renovated Barn with Tree House. Twenty minutes from Opryland and situated on 8 acres, this guest house is a renovated barn. The ground floor has a living room and a kitchen, and what used to be the hayloft is now a bedroom with a bath. The grounds feature a tree house that overlooks a creek, and the hostess doesn't charge for extra guests who bring their own bedding. *Represented by:* Nashville Bed & Breakfast, D-2704, (615) 327-4546. $44–$56.

Land, Lots of Land. Each of the guest rooms here opens onto a deck that overlooks a trout stream and the woods surrounding it. Both retired navy people, the hosts raise Tennessee walking horses, and if you know how to ride, there are 100 acres of land to do it on. *Represented by:* Nashville Bed & Breakfast, E-3701, (615) 327-4546. $25–$69.

Pride House

409 Broadway, Jefferson, TX 75657. (214) 665-2675. *Hostess:* Ruthmary Jordan.

Pride House is a Victorian building with stained-glass windows in every room. A certain Mr. Brown built the house for his daughter in 1888, and he used a great deal of hardwood in its construction. The trim, the cabinetry, the wainscoting, and the moldings are all testimony to Mr. Brown's love of wood (not to mention the fact that he owned a sawmill).

In addition to the rooms in the main house, guest accommodations are available in a small saltbox building that used to be a kitchen house. That house features a queen-size rope bed, the kitchen's original drainboard and flour bin, and an attic room with an antique desk, an Oriental rug, and walls hung with primitive watercolors.

Ruthmary's breakfast varies, sometimes including exotic melons, baked apples, or stuffed pears, and always including juices, homemade breads, jams, and coffee. Ruthmary, who used to run a restaurant, told me that her change of business was quite easy to make, adding, "I'm not professional at anything. I just do things 'cause I like 'em." Ruthmary likes running a bed-and-breakfast place.

Accommodations: 5 rooms with private bath. *Smoking:* Permitted. *Children:* Permitted. *Pets:* Not permitted. *Breakfast:* Included. *Driving Instructions:* From Route 59 take Route 49 (Broadway) east for five blocks.

Old Homestead Inn*

P.O. Box 35, Barnet, VT 05821. (802) 633-4100. *Hosts:* Robert and Mary Gordon.

Built around 1880, Old Homestead Inn is a large Colonial structure painted white with black shutters. A postman and a housekeeper, Robert and Mary Gordon dreamed of opening an inn; so they moved here from Long Island and did just that. Their house is situated on 22 acres thick with pine trees, and their property includes several streams and a waterfall.

The lounge and dining area have dark pine floors and reproduction Colonial furnishings. Mary's paintings, landscapes and seascapes influenced by Van Gogh and Gaugin, hang in the lounge area. Off the dining area there's a sun parlor with wooden walls, floors, and ceiling and with windows that overlook the mountains. The lounge area also has a bar, and Robert and Mary are happy to provide their guests with setups.

Two large guest rooms overlook the Connecticut River and the White Mountains and are furnished for the most part in oak. One room has an iron bed, a big old oblong antique mirror, and an oaken night table. Both rooms have wide-paneled maple floors, white quilts, and white ruffled curtains. They share a bath that has a pedestal sink and all of its old fixtures still intact.

Mary's breakfast includes juice, English muffins and freshly baked doughnuts, and coffee. For those with appetites still unsatisfied, Mary is willing "to make 'em something."

Accommodations: 5 rooms, 2 with private bath. *Smoking:* Permitted. *Children:* Permitted. *Pets:* Not permitted. *Breakfast:* Included. *Driving Instructions:* Old Homestead Inn is 10 miles south of St. Johnsbury on Route 5.

*Member: *American Bed and Breakfast Program.*

Woodruff House*

13 East Street, Barre, VT 05641. (802) 476-7745. *Hosts:* Robert R. and Terry L. Somiani.

The Woodruff House is an 1883 Queen Anne structure that was remodeled years later by a wealthy granite manufacturer. Across the street from a park, it is surrounded by a well-trimmed lawn with beds of flowers and numerous trees.

A large whitewashed stone fireplace, with a built-in bookcase below its mantel and an antique clock on top of it, dominates one of the living rooms, which also has a wrought-iron chandelier.

One guestroom has an oaken bed and dresser and a tiny-print Victorian wallpaper that matches the quilt and throw pillows. The sitting room is done in white wicker, with pillows covered in a colorful blue and green floral print, plants, and lacy curtains. The dining room has a large table usually set with fresh flowers, numerous hand-tooled antique chairs, and plenty of natural light.

The Woodruff House is close to the state capitol, the Kent Museum, and the world's largest granite quarries. Downhill skiing, cross-country skiing, and a variety of sports are all nearby.

Accommodations: 3 rooms, 1 with private bath. *Smoking:* Not permitted. *Children:* Permitted. *Pets:* Not permitted. *Breakfast:* Included. *Driving Instructions:* Near the center of Barre, adjacent to the park.

Brandon **VERMONT**

Stone Mill Farm*

P.O. Box 203, Brandon, VT 05733. (802) 247-6137. *Hosts:* Eileen and Charles Roeder.

Federal in design, Stone Mill Farm's main farmhouse was built in 1773 by Salmon Farr, who added a guest ell in 1786. The 10-acre grounds feature a swimming pool and a logging trail, which runs through cedars and ends at the third tee of the Neshoe Golf Course.

The Roeders raise pigs, chickens, ducks, and geese, who stroll or flap around the property. They also raise berries and make maple syrup.

The house is furnished with English and American antiques, a collection the Roeders assembled during Charles's previous career as an antiques dealer and auctioneer. One guest room, furnished in antiques and wicker, has double glass doors leading onto a balcony that overlooks the pool and the neighboring dairy Farm. The Roeders serve a complimentary breakfast on their porch.

Accommodations: 3 rooms, 1 with private bath. *Smoking:* Permitted. *Children:* Permitted. *Pets:* Not permitted. *Breakfast:* Included. *Driving Instructions:* Take Route 7 North; turn right on Route 73 East, then turn left on Diet Lane; cross the bridge and bear right.

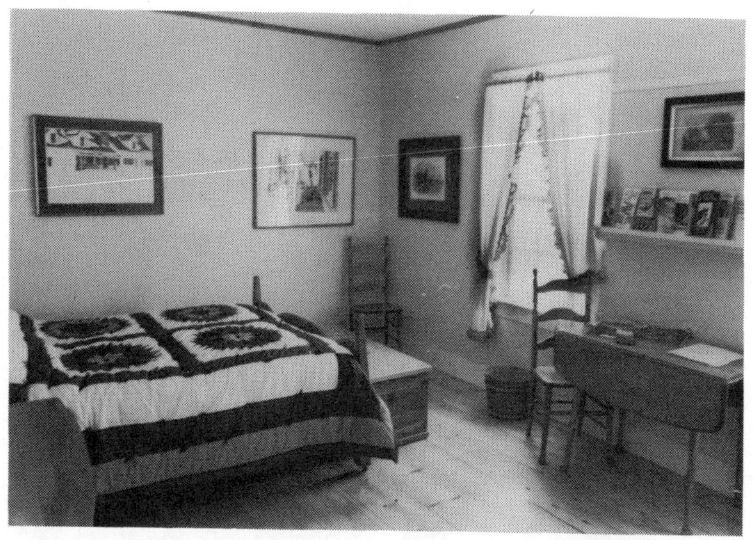

Gary-Meadows Farm*

R.R. 1, Craftsbury, VT 05826. (802) 586-2536. *Hostess:* Nicki Houston.

On 700 acres of land, Gary-Meadows Farm, a computerized dairy farm with 650 registered holstein cows, includes a rambling 1884 Cape Cod–style farmhouse with a Vermont-style sunparlor. Behind the house there's a still-water pond (fed entirely by rain) where guests may go fishing and boating.

The guest room, which is available from May through October, has wide-panel pine floors, light blue walls decorated with watercolors done by a friend of the Houstons', a large wooden bed covered by a brown, blue, and beige sunburst quilt, a drop-leaf maple table, two ladder-back chairs, a maple bureau and nighttable, and two large windows with twelve panes of glass each. The living room features a walnut Empire hutch and bureau, a walnut spool cabinet, and a series of braided rugs.

Nicki is an ex-teacher now in the process of raising three children, but she manages to find time to involve herself in the publicity activities of the Vermont Country Players, a local drama group, and to show people around her and her husband's farm.

On pressed-paint dishes, a breakfast large enough for any-

body appears each morning: Juice, homemade coffee cake or muffins, three kinds of cereal, homemade jams and jellies, and coffee are part of the fare.

Accommodations: 1 room with shared bath. *Smoking:* Permitted. *Children:* Permitted. *Pets:* Not permitted. *Breakfast:* Included. *Driving Instructions:* Gary-Meadows Farm is 1 mile from Craftsbury Village, 500 feet off Route 14 North.

House in the Wood*

R.F.D. Kirby Road, East Burke, VT 05832. (802) 626-9243.
Hosts: Jerry and Elaine Derry.

Built of four by fours, House in the Wood is a 1966 wooden-frame house. The entire structure has wooden walls and floors. Three rooms are done in butternut, one in white ash, one in brown ash, one in cherry, and the two bathrooms are done in oak. Where did all this wood come from? Host Jerry Derry, who designed the house, manages a sawmill.

The house has a 30- by 16-foot living room with seven windows that face Burke Mountain, which is a 3-minute drive from the house. The living room, carpeted wall to wall, is furnished with contemporary pieces and a few antiques such as an oaken secretary with a glass inset. There is also a large recreation room with a stone fireplace, a shuffleboard set, wall-to-wall carpeting, color television, and plenty of books. Three of the guest rooms have views of Burke Mountain. Guests are invited to use any part of the house they choose, including the kitchen.

Jerry and Elaine moved into their house four years ago and realized that the two of them didn't need so much room. Renting the three bedrooms worked out so well that they transformed their attached garage into another two guest rooms.

Accommodations: 5 rooms, 2 with private bath. *Smoking:* Permitted. *Children:* Permitted. *Pets:* Not permitted. *Driving Instructions:* House in the Wood is on Kirby Road ¾ mile north of East Burke Village.

*Member: *American Bed and Breakfast Program.*

Varnum's*

143 Weed Road, Essex Junction, VT 05452. (802) 899-4577. *Hosts:* Todd and Sheila Varnum.

Todd and Sheila Varnum have a large 1792 cedar shake farmhouse on more than 10 acres of land. One of the oldest buildings in the area, the Varnums' place, local legend has it, used to be a tavern that catered to the passengers of one of Vermont's stagecoach lines. The property is surrounded by mountains and affords a splendid view of Mount Mansfield.

One enters Varnum's through a large country kitchen, which has a wood-burning stove and an inexhaustible supply of hot chocolate. From there one passes through a dining room and a study to enter an 18- by 33-foot living room, which has traditional furniture, ruffled curtains, and a piano.

The guest rooms are off the upstairs hallway, which has a floor of 18-inch-wide pine boards (hidden beneath plywood until recently). One guest room, done in reds, features a reproduction antique pine bed covered with a handmade quilt; and the other room, done in yellows, has an antique brass-and-iron bed.

Also off the upstairs hallway is the Varnums' spa room, which has a passive solar shower and a hot tub that seats six. This room has lots of plants and an entire wall of windows looking out on trees and mountains.

Accommodations: 2 rooms with shared bath. *Smoking:* Not permitted. *Children:* Not permitted. *Pets:* Not permitted. *Breakfast:* Included. *Driving Instructions:* From Essex Junction, take Route 15 east 5.7 miles, and turn left on the dirt road. Varnum's is the first house on the left. The name is on the mailbox.

Foggy Hollow Farm*

Route 104, Fairfax, VT 05454. (802) 849-6385. *Hosts:* Mr. and Mrs. Jean-Paul Bouthillette.

A working dairy farm with some seventy-five cows, Foggy Hollow Farm consists of 400 acres of land. The farmhouse was constructed sometime around 1857 and later had the distinction of being the first home in the area to be wired for electricity.

The entire farmhouse is furnished in antiques, and the ambience is substantially enhanced by the many craft pieces Mrs. Bouthillette made. Her repertoire of skills includes sewing, embroidery, millinery, patchwork, and macramé. The house is filled with plants suspended in macramé hangers.

One guest room has an antique iron bed, an oaken night table and an oaken dresser, and a brown, peach, and beige carpet. The other contains an old maple bed, a sprinkling of antique furnishings, and a navy blue and white carpet. The walls are covered with a delicate brown-on-beige calico print wallpaper. The beds are covered with ruffled spreads.

Mrs. Bouthillette told me that in addition to her other skills, she is also a hair stylist, although I never found out whether or not she practices that skill on guests. "I do a little bit of everything," said she.

Accommodations: 2 rooms with shared bath. *Smoking:* Not permitted. *Children:* Permitted. *Pets:* Not permitted. *Breakfast:* Included. *Driving Instructions:* Take I-89 to the St. Albans exit, then pick up Route 104 East; proceed for 8 miles—it's the white house with black shutters.

Shady Rest*

R.F.D. 1, Fairfax, VT 05454. (802) 524-4395. *Hosts:* Euclide and Florence Magnan.

Situated on 30 acres of land filled with maple trees, 5 miles from Lake Champlain, Shady Rest is a *circa*-1880 Colonial structure painted white with green shutters. The surrounding area has many farms, and horses can be seen in the field across the road. The fall foliage season is particularly beautiful hereabouts.

The family room features maple floors, an antique oaken bureau, a maple table, a cherry grandfather clock, and beige wallpaper with a tiny print pattern. The living room has pine floors, a piano made of cherry, two cherry coffee tables, and a matching Queen Anne couch and loveseat, both of them covered by a pale cream fabric with a floral pattern in soft blues and yellows.

One guest room overlooks Lake Champlain and has white-painted furniture such as an antique trunk and a spool bed covered by a mint-green ruffled spread. The room has a wicker chair, painted a soft green, and white ruffled curtains at its three large windows.

Euclide and Florence have a large yard with picnic facilities, as well as a garden with geraniums, petunias, and blue hydrangeas.

Accommodations: 2 rooms with shared bath. *Smoking:* Not permitted. *Children:* Permitted. *Pets:* Permitted. *Breakfast:* Included. *Driving Instructions:* Shady Rest is on Route 104, 4 miles south of St. Albans.

Fair Meadows Farm Bed and Breakfast*

Route 235, Franklin, VT 05457. (802) 285-2132. *Hosts:* Phil and Terry Pierce.

Fair Meadows Farm has been in Phil Pierce's family since 1853. A fire some years after that destroyed the farmhouse, but the family rebuilt it in 1896. Phil and Terry still have the only piece of furniture that survived the blaze—a parlor chair with a wicker seat.

Fair Meadows is a 480-acre working dairy farm, so don't be surprised if you run into a cow while you're taking a stroll around the property. The Pierces' land has two ponds, but the animals have them pretty well tied up, which is to say that the ponds are more for seeing than for swimming.

The guest rooms are furnished with a mixture of heirloom antiques and contemporary pieces, and each room has at least two windows, which overlook the Green Mountains, the farm's rolling hills, and the plethora of big old maple trees that surround the house and the dairy barn. The guest-room floors are particularly interesting: Phil and Terry arranged carpet remnants into what you might call mosaics. The guest rooms are filled with green plants, of which the house contains more than a hundred.

The living room, carpeted in shades of green, is comfortably furnished and contains a television set guests are invited to watch. (The Pierces will lend a portable set to guests who crave late-night movies).

Breakfast is a treat: You can choose from bacon and eggs, blueberry muffins, pancakes, and french toast, the last two served with real maple syrup.

Accommodations: 3 rooms with shared bath. *Smoking:* Permitted. *Children:* Permitted. *Pets:* Permitted if well behaved. *Breakfast:* Included. *Driving Instructions:* Take Route 89 north to the Swanton exit, turn right, proceed 4 miles, turn left after Nadeau's Grocery, and go 8.1 more miles.

*Member: *American Bed and Breakfast Program.*

The Hayes House

Grafton, VT 05146. (802) 843-2461. *Hostess:* Margery Hayes Heindel.

In addition to running a guest house and raising Chesapeake Bay retrievers, Margery is currently serving her fifth term as chairman of Grafton's Board of Selectmen, a local elected body with the powers of a mayor. Her house is an 1803 shingled clapboard farmhouse on land that used to contain two sawmills, both constructed about 1793. The house has two porches.

Margery's living room overlooks a field, a garden, and a covered bridge that spans the Saxtons River. The focal point of the room is a brick fireplace with a fieldstone hearth. Other features are a three-legged coffee table whose top is a 4-inch-thick slab of teak, a Second Empire–period couch with carved swan heads and velvet upholstery, a brass coffee table from India, and a maroon Oriental rug with a floral design in various shades of blue. The room's ambience reflects Margery's having lived for several years in the Orient; and the stone rubbings she made while in Thailand, which hang in this room and others, suggest her eclectic—Oriental and traditional—taste in decor.

One guest room has a corner fireplace with a fieldstone hearth, an antique rope bed with a matching chest of drawers, wide-board pine floors, and a countercross-stitch floral bouquet on the wall.

Margery's breakfasts include homemade muffins, bread, and jellies, and she keeps a pot of soup on her stove in winter.

Accommodations: 4 rooms, 1 with private bath. *Smoking:* Permitted except in bedrooms. *Children:* Permitted. *Pets:* Dogs Permitted. *Breakfast:* Included. *Driving Instructions:* The house is in the town of Grafton, near the covered bridge.

Randolph **VERMONT**

Windover House

R.F.D. 2, Randolph, VT 05060. (802) 728-3802. *Hosts:* George and Shirley Carlisle.

Windover House used to be called the Mid-State Villa, after geologists had ascertained that this 1800 New England farmhouse stood on the exact geographic center of Vermont and a statewide contest had been held to find a name for it. Curiously enough, this house feels like the very center of Vermont when you're relaxing on its terrace and contemplating the 5 wooded acres that surround it. The Carlisles have some of the oldest trees in Vermont on their property. The lounge, which looks onto the terrace, has cherry paneling, a fireplace, and a color television set, and there is an enclosed porch with a fireplace and an outer terrace. Each light and airy guest room has a fine view.

Although the Carlisles don't serve complimentary meals, they offer a sort of cafeteria to guests, who can make themselves coffee or tea whenever they like.

Accommodations: 8 rooms with shared baths. *Smoking:* Permitted. *Children:* Permitted. *Pets:* Not permitted. *Driving Instructions:* Take Route I-89 to exit 4. Turn left, and go 1¼ miles to Randolph Drive. Turn right at the Windover House sign, and continue to the corner.

Guest House Christel Horman

Mountain Road, Stowe, VT 05672. *Mailing Address:* R.R. 1, Box 1635, Stowe, VT 05672. (802) 253-4846. *Hosts:* Christel and Jim Horman.

Built in 1980, Christel and Jim's house looks like a large Swiss chalet. A balcony encircles the entire house, situated among pine trees in the beautiful Green Mountains. The grounds contain an outdoor swimming pool, lawn games, and a trout stream. When it's cold, you can begin cross-country skiing from the Hormans' front door; or you can drive 10 minutes to Stowe, one of the Northeast's best downhill-skiing areas.

All guest rooms have private baths, two double beds, wall-to-wall carpeting, and individually controlled thermostats. The parlor—where guests congregate for coffee or hot apple cider and exchange stories of frozen slopes or fish that got away—has a fireplace, wall-to-wall carpeting, contemporary early American furniture, and plenty of books and magazines. The Hormans offer a full complimentary country breakfast.

Accommodations: 8 rooms with private bath. *Smoking:* Tolerated. *Children:* Permitted. *Pets:* Not permitted. *Breakfast:* Included. *Driving Instructions:* Take Route I-89 to Waterbury; take exit 10 toward Stowe; turn left at the traffic light onto Mountain Road (Route 108) and proceed 6 miles.

Birch Wood by the Mountain

Box 80, German Flats Road, Warren, VT 05674. (802) 583-2100. *Hosts:* Kathleen and John Horst.

Surrounded, as its name implies, by birch trees, Birch Wood by the Mountain is a 1964 Tyrolean-style chalet that was constructed soon after the opening of the Sugarbush ski area, a five-minute drive from the house. It originally served as a winter vacation home for Kathleen and John, but when they moved here permanently in 1970, they decided to share the place with fellow skiers and sailplane pilots, who catch the Green Mountain thermals and whoosh overhead from time to time.

The living room has a fireplace with a pine mantel, bittersweet wall-to-wall carpeting, color television, a stereo, and two overstuffed couches whose upholstery echos the colors in Van Gogh's *Sunflowers,* a reproduction of which hangs on the living room wall. The living room contains a dining area with a walnut table and a matching china closet. You can see several of Sugarbush's ski trails through the living-room windows. The guest rooms have queen-size twin beds, maple dressers and chairs, and views of the Mad River Valley.

At cocktail time Kathleen and John serve their guests fresh apple cider and cheese (in winter by the fire, during warm weather on the deck, which is encircled by woods). The Warren area is as beautiful a spot as I've ever seen, and the more so if you're adventurous enough to view it from a glider, which is a popular way of sightseeing around here.

Accommodations: 3 rooms with shared bath. *Smoking:* Permitted. *Children:* Permitted. *Pets:* Not permitted. *Breakfast:* Included during the winter. *Driving Instructions:* From Waitsfield, go west on Route 17 for 2 miles to the junction with German Flats Road; cross over the small bridge on German Flats Road, and continue for 3 more miles.

Schneider Haus*

Route 100, Box 283A, Waterbury, VT 05676. (802) 244-7726. *Hosts:* George and Irene Ballschneider.

Well back from the highway and surrounded by forested mountains, Schneider Haus is a Tyrolean-style chalet that George and Irene Ballschneider built by themselves. They picked out and carried home each stone in their fireplace; they dragged lumber to the building site with a snowmobile. It took them two and a half years to build their chalet, with monies they received from the sale of their New York City delicatessen. "I wanted a house like one of those hideaways you find in the Austrian Mountains," says Irene.

Each guest room, beautifully furnished with early American antiques and period reproductions, has a door leading to the balcony that wraps around the entire house. In addition to its huge stone fireplace, the lounge has 21 feet of windows overlooking brilliant foliage or knee-deep snow or summer forests you can't see for the trees. George and Irene also offer tennis courts, a color television set, a sauna, and cows and chickens and a game room for the children.

Accommodations: 10 rooms, 2 with private bath. *Smoking:* Permitted. *Children:* Over 4 permitted. *Pets:* Not permitted. *Breakfast:* Included. *Driving Instructions:* Proceeding southward from Waterbury on Route I-89, take exit 10 5 miles south of Waterbury.

Becket's Run. Becket's Run is a rustic cottage on a farm 12 miles northwest of Charlottesville. The cottage contains a sitting room, a bath, a kitchen, and a bedroom. The living room has a free-standing fireplace around which the owners pile plenty of wood. Your hosts have a thoroughbred horse; through the cottage's large windows and screened-in porch you can usually see it grazing in a picturesque pasture. *Represented by:* Guesthouses Bed & Breakfast, (804) 979-7264 or (804) 979-8327. $75.

Chaumine. On top of a mountain 9 miles west of Charlottesville, Chaumine is a contemporary wood, stone, and glass cottage. The living room/dining room, bath, and kitchen are around a massive stone fireplace. From a deck you can see woods. Two bedrooms, a double and a king-size, are available. *Represented by:* Guesthouses Bed & Breakfast, (804) 979-7264. $84–$128.

L'Abri. L'Abri is a cypress cottage in the wooded mountains 8 miles southeast of Charlottesville. Decorated with antiques, it has a living room/dining room, a complete kitchen, a bath, a bedroom, and a patio. The bath overlooks a pine grove, and the living room opens onto a kidney-shaped pool. The refrigerator is stocked with muffins, jam, and juice. *Represented by:* Guesthouses Bed & Breakfast, (804) 979-7264. $75.

Windhaven Farm. Overlooking the Blue Ridge Mountains, Windhaven Farm offers accommodation in a private wing of a recently constructed Georgian-style home. The guest wing has a country kitchen with a wood stove, two bedrooms, a bath, and a deck. There are stables for those who bring horses, and guests can arrange to use a hot tub. *Represented by:* Guesthouses Bed & Breakfast, (804) 979-7264. $100.

Sassafras Hill. Sassafras Hill is an old farmhouse in the foothills of the Blue Ridge Mountains, 3 miles northeast of Charlottesville. There are small farm animals, a vegetable garden, and a pond for fishing. The house has two bedrooms, a bath, a dining room, a living room, a study, and a kitchen with a wood stove. *Represented by:* Guesthouses Bed & Breakfast, (804) 979-7264. $75–$100.

Coleman Cottage. Coleman Cottage is a redecorated servants' house on Seven Oaks Farm, an antebellum estate 15 miles west of Charlottesville. At the base of Afton Mountain (the junction of the Skyline Drive and the Blue Ridge Parkway), the

Above: Coleman Cottage (*Guesthouses Bed & Breakfast*)

Casa Maria (*Guesthouses Bed & Breakfast*)

cottage features three bedrooms, living and dining rooms, a kitchen, a bath, and two porches with views of the spacious grounds and the surrounding mountains. *Represented by:* Guest-houses Bed & Breakfast, (804) 979-7264. $80–$210.

Lakefront Home. The spacious hexagonal Great Room of this accommodation offers views of Monticello Lake from three angles. This home, 30 minutes from Charlottesville, has a 60-foot deck, wall-to-wall carpeting, three bedrooms, a fireplace, and air conditioning. *Represented by:* Guesthouses Bed & Breakfast, (804) 979-7264. Weekly only—$400–$700.

Bavarian-style House. This split-level Bavarian-style house is 16 miles west of Charlottesville, in the Blue Ridge foothills. Each of its two guest rooms opens onto a back patio. The house is furnished mainly with antiques. *Represented by:* Guesthouses Bed & Breakfast, (804) 979-7264. $44–$80.

Japanese House. Although the roof of this Japanese-style house looks thatched, it is actually made of cleverly laid-out hand-split cedar shakes. The master bedroom has a king-size bed; the master bath, a sunken tub. The grounds, which were on the 1974 Virginia Garden Tour, feature a private tennis court. *Represented by:* Guesthouses Bed & Breakfast, (804) 979-7264. $60–$80.

Melrose. Halfway between Charlottesville and the Skyline Drive, this home is a composite of two eighteenth-century structures, *circa* 1738 and 1797, that were dismantled, moved, and reassembled. The guest suite has a private entrance and hallway, a fireplace, eighteenth-century paneling, kitchen privileges, and the use of a balcony overlooking the grounds, which were on the 1979 Virginia Garden Tour. *Represented by:* Guesthouses Bed & Breakfast, (804) 979-7264. $55–$65.

Casa Maria. On 27 acres that overlook the Blue Ridge Mountains, this Mediterranean-style stucco structure was built in 1921. The grounds contain several patios and gardens, and the surrounding area, mostly woods and fields, features some particularly fine stone work. Each guest suite has a fireplace. *Represented by:* Guesthouses Bed & Breakfast, (804) 979-7264. $48–$60.

Georgian. This large Georgian home was built in the early 1900s for the first president of the University of Virginia. A physician and his wife, your hosts, have daily help and make sure that Southern hospitality lives on. *Represented by:* Guesthouses Bed & Breakfast, (804) 979-7264. $48.

Slave Quarters Suite. This guest suite, upstairs in the former slave quarters, consists of a sitting room and two bedrooms. Your hosts, an antique dealer and his wife, have furnished their home with a combination of antiques and contemporary pieces and maintain a bonzai garden. Private entrance. *Represented by:* Guesthouses Bed & Breakfast, (804) 979-7264. $44–$48.

Ednam. Conveniently as well as scenically located, this brick split-level home overlooks the Boar's Head Inn. Guest quarters have doors leading onto a patio with a private entrance. Each guest room has a private bath and shares a recreation room that has a fireplace. *Represented by:* Guesthouses Bed & Breakfast, (804) 979-7264. $48.

Bellair. This French country home 2 miles west of the University of Virginia has a garden, a heated pool, and two guest rooms, one with a private entrance. *Represented by:* Guesthouses Bed & Breakfast, (804) 979-7264. $48.

Upstairs Apartment. This Colonial-style home next to the University of Virginia has two bedrooms available for guests. It also has a hot tub, hidden by bushes in the garden, that guests may reserve. One bedroom has a four-poster and a fireplace. *Represented by:* Guesthouses Bed & Breakfast, (804) 979-7264. $75–$125.

(*Guesthouses Bed & Breakfast*)

Historic Church Hill. This 1870s Victorian structure features four working fireplaces, exposed wood and brick walls, and several skylights. Filled with plants, the house contains baskets and other craft pieces from all over the world, especially from Brazil, a past home of the owner. Your hostess, a snorkler and shell collector, draws finely detailed studies of pine cones, shells, and other natural phenomena. This home has been featured on the Church Hill Tour. *Represented by:* Bensonhouse of Richmond, (804) 321-6277 or 649-4601. $28–$32.

Ginter Park. Not quite as tall as the stately old magnolia that dominates its front yard, this 1920s two-story white frame house has a slate roof, an arched fireplace in the living room, double crown moldings in the living and dining rooms, and brass fixtures almost everywhere. Your hostess, a woman whose interests include duplicate bridge and canoeing, serves homemade bread with her complimentary breakfast. *Represented by:* Bensonhouse of Richmond, (804) 321-6277 or 649-4601. $28–$32.

Hanover County. A 1790 clapboard cottage, not far from the main house on a 200-acre estate, this accommodation consists of three rooms on three levels, each with a fireplace. Furnished with antiques, the cottage has a kitchen area with exposed brick walls, an 1800 yellow-pine painted bed, thick monogrammed towels, and maid service on weekdays. Your hosts, competitive snow-skiers with careers in real estate and insurance, invite guests to use the estate's swimming pool. *Represented by:* Bensonhouse of Richmond, (804) 321-6277 or 649-4601. $80–*$100.*

Fan Area. Maple and mahogany and oak woodwork, stained-glass windows, 11-foot ceilings, bay windows—appointments like these characterize this early-twentieth-century Queen Anne structure that overlooks Richmond's West Grace Street. The hexagonal kitchen has heavy carved paneling and exposed brick there. The bedroom, its bay windows overlooking West Grace Street, has a fireplace with an oak mantel and French doors that open onto a living room with barn-sided walls and another fireplace. Your hosts make breakfast to order. *Represented by:* Bensonhouse of Richmond, (804) 321-6277 or 649-4601. Rates on request.

Historic Fan District. This 1914 red-brick structure was designed by Duncan Lee, a turn-of-the-century Richmond architect. The garden room has a marble floor, and furnishings throughout are a blend of genuine antiques and period reproductions. To complement the traditional furnishings, your host has used unusual window treatments that create an open and airy effect, and has added to the decor colorful works of contemporary art. Currently in real estate, he has lived in France, Newfoundland, and New York. A skier and traveler, he has been involved in a number of Fan District renovations. *Represented by:* Bensonhouse of Richmond, (804) 321-6277 or 649-4601. $40–$50.

Clark Row. In 1900, Maben Clark, an early twentieth-century photographer, built four connecting houses known now as The Clark Row. This home is one of these and features stained glass and old chandeliers, hollyberry-red walls in the living rooms, and fine woodwork throughout. Your hosts, university professors, are urban archeologists who have gathered a collection of aged wood—weathered gable peaks, porch posts, fretwork, and so on. They have also gathered a collection of cats. *Represented by:* Bensonhouse of Richmond, (804) 321-6277 or 649-4601. $32–$40.

Monument Avenue. Some of the furnishings in this 1924, cottage-style house were acquired at the 1922 Vacanzati Palace sale in Florence, Italy. Among the heirlooms here are genuine Renaissance pieces including tapestries and rugs. The main rooms have Art Deco cornices with a running design of vines or flowers, and each opens through French doors onto the marble-paved loggia (now enclosed) or the garden. *Represented by:* Bensonhouse of Richmond, (804) 321-6277 or 649-4601. $40–$50.

Ginter Park. The main house, which has columns in front and crepe myrtle and magnolias surrounding it, was built in 1924; the log cabin on the other side of a grape arbor and the gardens was built sometime later. The cabin's interior is mortar and log, the beams are exposed, and the bedroom has a fireplace. There is a greatroom with a stone hearth and also a kitchen and a bath. Your hosts, both college professors, he in medical research and she in the liberal arts, offer guests accommodations in both the main house and the cottage. *Represented by:* Bensonhouse of Richmond, (804) 321-6277 or 649-4601. Rates on request.

Fan District. Previously inhabited by a fundamentalist preacher and a motorcycle gang rumored to have ridden their bikes up the front steps, this 1907 frame house is now occupied by an elementary-school librarian and a faculty member of a university's business school. The furnishings are a blend of antique and traditional, and appointments include wood-grained fireplace mantels, cut-crystal shelving, and walls hung generously with photographs and art. *Represented by:* Bensonhouse of Richmond, (804) 321-6277 or 649-4601. $40–$50.

NOTE: For a fee, Bensonhouse of Richmond can arrange for their guests to have a luxurious breakfast in bed—bamboo trays, linen napkins, a complimentary bottle of champagne, smoked salmon, quiche lorraine, chocolates for the ladies and cigars for the gentlemen—all this served by a man in a tuxedo and a woman in a French maid's outfit.

Fan District (*Bensonhouse of Richmond*)

Battleground. Looking forward to play, this young family, which includes two small children, welcomes guests with young children of their own. Their home, a contemporary one on 5 secluded and wooded acres, is 45 minutes from Portland, Oregon. *Represented by:* Northwest Bed & Breakfast, #108, (503) 246-8366 or 246-2383. $18–$34.

Bothell. This modern home beside a forested golf course features a wood-burning fireplace, a wet bar, and a putting green. A large patio is available for use by guests, as are a color television set and a stereo radio. *Represented by:* Northwest Bed & Breakfast, #164, (503) 246-8366 or 246-2383. $22–$34.

Bremerton. This home features 200 feet of waterfront immediately outside the front door and a spectacular view of Mount Rainier. The hosts, who enjoy fishing and boating, welcome teenagers. *Represented by:* Northwest Bed & Breakfast, #104, (503) 246-8366 or 246-2383. $20–$34.

Burien. Surrounded by gardens and lawns, this New England-style structure has a living room with a cathedral-style ceiling, a balcony, and an antique pump organ. The hosts, professional people, are involved in church activities and enjoy gardening and playing pool. *Represented by:* Northwest Bed & Breakfast, #152, (503) 246-8366 or 246-2383. $18–$30.

Chinook. Close to historic Astoria, this 1912 architect-designed home is situated in a parklike setting. Better still, perhaps, the host is a master chef. *Represented by:* Northwest Bed & Breakfast, #121 (503) 246-8366 or 246-2383. $22–$30.

East Bellevue. The host here raises horses, and experienced riders can take advantage of this and gallop around if they like. Guests cannot, however, ride the cats and dogs that share this rambling rural house. *Represented by:* Northwest Bed & Breakfast, #160, (503) 246-8366 or 246-2383. $15.

East Bellevue. Only 15 minutes from the center of Seattle, this Tyrolean-style chalet is surrounded by woods. A management consultant and an artist, the hosts speak Spanish, French, German, and some Scandinavian languages, as well as English. Hiking trails and horses are available in a nearby park. *Represented by:* Northwest Bed & Breakfast, #161, (503) 246-8366 or 246-2383. $22–$34.

Kirkland. Thirty minutes from the center of Seattle, this contemporary home, furnished with antiques, has hosts who enjoy music, art, politics, and a lively game of pinochle or backgammon. The hosts speak a little Yiddish and invite their guests to take part in the Friday Sabbath ceremony. *Represented by:* Northwest Bed & Breakfast, #158, (503) 246-8366 or 246-2383. $22–$35.

Northwest Seattle. Built of natural woods, this ultramodern house has a deck overlooking a marina, as well as Puget Sound and the Olympic Mountains. The house, a half hour from the center of Seattle, is close to Golden Gardens and Swimming Beach. *Represented by:* Northwest Bed & Breakfast, #156, (503) 246-8366 or 246-2383. $18–$34.

Ocean Park. Your hosts, Canadian and Scottish, can arrange for those who desire it a private visit to Cape Disappointment Lighthouse. Their house, a modern one surrounded by pine trees, is a short walk, over sand dunes, from the beach. Children are welcome, and if you find clams on the beach, your hosts will gladly cook them for you. *Represented by:* Northwest Bed & Breakfast, #120, (503) 246-8366 or 246-2383. $18–$34.

Olympia. This large 56-year-old house on 2.5 wooded acres adjacent to Puget Sound features easy access to a beach and a view of Mount Rainier. Public-health professionals, the hosts are enamored of classical music, cooking, and wines. *Represented by:* Northwest Bed & Breakfast, #106, (503) 246-8366 or 246-2383. $18–$34.

Seattle. Your hosts—conversant in French and fond of opera, sports and travel—have a contemporary home that affords spectacular views of Lake Washington. The bedroom has a television set, and the hosts are willing to pick guests up at the airport. *Represented by:* Northwest Bed & Breakfast, #150, (503) 246-8366 or 246-2383. $18–$25.

Seattle. Your host, a real estate broker interested in the visual and performing arts and interior design, has a 1929 Tudor-style house with a large deck overlooking Lake Washington and the Cascades. The house features a private dock, and experienced sailors are welcome to sail in the host's small boat. *Represented by:* Northwest Bed & Breakfast, #151 (503) 246-8366 or 246-2383. $20–$25.

University. Involved in community activities, your host is a

French chef who speaks—besides fluent French and English—some German, Italian, and Spanish. His recently restored Edwardian home, furnished with period pieces, offers two rooms for guests. The house is immediately across a boulevard from a large city park. *Represented by:* Northwest Bed & Breakfast, #154, (503) 246-8366 or 246-2383. $20–$34.

Seattle (*Northwest Bed & Breakfast* #152)

Bellevue (*Northwest Bed & Breakfast* #161)

The James House

1238 Washington Street, Port Townsend, WA 98368. (206) 385-1238. *Hosts:* Rod, Deb, and Storey La Montagne.

An 1889 Victorian structure, the James House was built by Francis Wilcox James, a wealthy English capitalist who had careers as a customs inspector, an Indian agent, and an assistant lighthouse keeper. Mr. James built the house to retire in, but his wife died just seven weeks after the two of them moved in. Not a man enamored of spending time alone, Mr. James, shortly after his loss, married his housekeeper, a 24-year-old woman 53 years his junior. The marriage later ended in divorce.

The house that Mr. James built has sweeping views of Port Townsend, Mount Rainier, Quimpec Sound, and the Cascades. It contains such stuff as ornately carved fireplaces in both the parlor and the library, parquet floors fashioned of oak, walnut, and cherry, and carved brass door hinges.

What used to be the master bedroom is now the bridal suite: a pair of rooms with parquet floors, a fireplace, a small private balcony, and a view of Puget Sound. The guest rooms, most of which have water or mountain views or both, are decorated with antiques and plants. Among the accommodations to choose from are two garden suites, one with a wood-burning stove, each of which has two rooms and views of the water.

Accommodations: 12 rooms, 4 with private bath. *Smoking:* Permitted. *Children:* Under twelve not permitted. *Pets:* Not permitted. *Breakfast:* Included. *Driving Instructions:* The James House is on the bluffs in Port Townsend.

Lizzie's

731 Pierce Street, Port Townsend, WA 98368. (206) 385-4168 or (206) 385-9826. *Hostess:* Thelma Scudi.

Lizzie's is an 1887 Italianate mansion secluded by hedges and shaded by mature plantings such as a pear tree and a plum tree that are as old as the house. Pear butter and plum preserves are always available at Lizzie's, which is owned and operated by Thelma Scudi, whose careers have included running a construction company, working in the aerospace industry, and designing kitchens.

Thelma once owned an antique business, which perhaps explains how she managed to acquire some of her furnishings. The parlor has a Chinese red wall-to-wall carpet, a hand-painted metal fireplace with a navy blue leather Chesterfield couch facing it, a red leather Chippendale wing chair, and a Queen Anne wing chair and ottoman upholstered in a navy and cream blazed chintz. The room has its original wall and ceiling papers, a Knabe rosewood grand piano, and on either side of the fireplace a tapestry that came from the original production of *Flower Drum Song.* A life-size statue of a Chinese temple guard watches over all of this, and so does Thelma, whose conversation I recommend.

The rooms, most of them with water views, are furnished with antiques, and Thelma has a local chemist make glycerine soaps and apricot lotions and bubble baths for her guests.

Breakfast here includes fresh fruit, yogurt, brown eggs cooked in their shells, hot breads, and homemade preserves.

Accommodations: 8 rooms, 2 with private bath. *Smoking:* Permitted. *Children:* Permitted "if they can function graciously in an adult environment." *Pets:* Not permitted. *Breakfast:* Included. *Driving Instructions:* Lizzie's is one block from Puget Sound and six blocks from the Port Townsend bluffs.

40 Acres of Parkland (*Alberta Bed and Breakfast*)

Country Living (*Alberta Bed & Breakfast*)

CANADA

ALBERTA

*40 Acres of **Parkland.*** Twenty minutes from downtown Edmonton, this contemporary home has a backyard that's contiguous with 40 acres of parkland. The park has a man-made lake stocked each year with trout, which are yours to take and eat if you can catch them. In winter, guests can ski cross-country or skate on the lake. The hosts enjoy taking guests on tours and will arrange for a baby-sitter or baby-sit themselves. *Represented by:* Alberta Bed & Breakfast, (403) 462-8885. $20–$35.

Two-Bedroom Suite. This contemporary home is in a quiet residential neighborhood, 20 minutes by public transportation from downtown Edmonton. The house has a large garden and a patio, both of which guests are invited to use, and the guest suite has two bedrooms, a rumpus room with a Hide-a-Bed, a private bath, and a private entrance. *Represented by:* Alberta Bed & Breakfast, (403) 462-8885. $20–$35.

Country Living. Situated in the wide-open spaces, this contemporary home has a small greenhouse beside it and numerous bird feeders, which are easily seen through the house's many large windows. The guest room, done in yellows and golds, has a private bath. There's plenty of room on the property for guests to bring along a trailer or a boat. *Represented by:* Alberta Bed & Breakfast, (403) 462-8885. $20–$35.

Airport Pickup. The host, the director of the local Senior Citizen Day Centre, is willing to pick guests up at the airport and also to conduct tours and arrange for baby-sitting or do it himself. Three guest rooms are available, one with a private bath. Public transportation stops at the front door. *Represented by:* Alberta Bed & Breakfast, (403) 462-8885. $20–$35.

Surrey. These accommodations—one room with a double bed and one with twins—are in a suburban neighborhood slightly south of Vancouver. Guests are invited to use the swimming pool and the television set. The hosts' interests include natural foods, preventive health practices, and spinning. *Represented by:* Northwest Bed & Breakfast, #920, (503) 246-8366 or 246-2383. $12–$25.

Vancouver Island. Your host, a devotee of music and antique collecting, has an Edwardian-style home surrounded by gardens. One guest room contains a king-sized bed, and the other (available May through August) has a brass double bed, a sitting area, and a balcony. *Represented by:* Northwest Bed & Breakfast, #950, (503) 246-8366 or 246-2383. $22–$34.

Third Avenue near Alma. Mrs. Darragh offers guests a large bedroom that opens onto a rear garden. This accommodation, one block from a bus stop, is convenient to beaches, the University of British Columbia, and the planetarium. Mrs. Darragh offers a Continental breakfast and, if you check with her in advance, may well let you bring your pet. Call Mrs. Darragh, (604) 224-3854. Member of Town & Country Bed & Breakfast in B.C. $20–$35.

Granville near West Fifty-eighth. A two-story Bungalow-style house, this accommodation is a guest suite with two bedrooms, a kitchen and dining area, and a recreation room with a fireplace and simple but comfortable couches and chairs. Guests are invited to use the house's laundry facilities, as well as the wading pool in the garden. Convenient to shops and restaurants, this guest house is only twenty minutes west of downtown Vancouver by public transportation. Pets are welcome. Call Mrs. Mooney (604) 263-6517. Member of Town & Country Bed & Breakfast in B.C. $25–$40.

Twenty-seventh Avenue near McKenzie. Mrs. Smith, a Scotswoman, has a 1945 West coast-style house surrounded by evergreens, birches, poplars, and a garden. There is a large patio on the grounds and the house has a spacious deck that overlooks the city. From elsewhere in the house there are views of the mountains and the ocean. The guest quarters consist of a bedroom with a private bath and a private entrance, and guests may use the recreation room, with its fireplace, books, games, small pool table, and television. Call Mrs. Smith, (604) 738-9160. Member of Town & Country Bed & Breakfast in B.C. \$25–\$40.

Ladner. Featured in a promotional film about bed-and-breakfast places, this guest house recently received a Heritage Restoration Award. Host Joan Hoar has a Victorian farmhouse, as well as a barn, situated on 200 acres. One guest room has a view of fields; and the other, a view of the mountains. The house, simply but comfortably furnished, is 5 minutes from the Victoria Ferry to Vancouver Island. Call Joan Hoar, (604) 946-7886. Member of Town & Country Bed & Breakfast in B.C. \$30.

Mountroyal and Skyline. Perched at the 900-foot level of Grouse Mountain, this guest house features a great deal of glass and a wraparound balcony that overlooks Vancouver and the harbor from the north. The house, which has something of an Oriental feeling about it, was designed by one of the hosts, an engineer. The living room has 12-foot ceilings, and the entrance hall has cathedral ceilings. You can walk to the Grouse Mountain Skyride from here, and the Baden Powell Trail is a mile away. Call Mrs. Copes, (604) 987-8988. Member of Town & Country Bed & Breakfast in B.C. \$20–\$30.

Cliffridge and Clements. Twenty minutes north of downtown Vancouver and 5 minutes from the ocean, this contemporary house offers guests a combined bedroom and sitting area with a brick fireplace that has a slate hearth. The walls are wood-paneled, the floor is covered with a red shag carpet, and the room overlooks the garden, which has rhododendrons, an azalea bush, and large hedges. The house is in a scenic area near a salmon hatchery. Call Mrs. Hansen, (604) 988-5307. Member of Town & Country Bed & Breakfast in B.C. \$20–\$30.

St. James and Mahon. Architecturally something of a Colonial structure, this guest house has three rooms for guests. Decorated primarily in yellows, two of the rooms have views of the garden (planted with roses, rhododendrons, begonias, and geraniums), and the other room, which has a fireplace, faces the mountains. There's public recreation two blocks from the house—a pool, a sauna, tennis courts, and other recreational facilities are available to guests. Call Mr. or Mrs. Poole, (604) 987-4594. Member of Town & Country Bed & Breakfast in B.C. \$35.

OVERNIGHT
LODGING

Bread and Roses

82 Victoria Street, Annapolis Royal, Nova Scotia, Canada BOS 1A0. (902) 532-5727. *Hosts:* John and Barbara Taylor.

When women textile workers early in this century organized a strike so that they could work 54 instead of 56 hours a week, James Openheim wrote a poem about their struggle. "Bread and Roses" passionately asserts that people need beauty and inspiration as well as life's necessities. Bread and Roses—an 1882 Queen Anne structure with a roof made of Welsh slate—took its name from both the title and the message of Openheim's poem.

The entranceway has a floor of mahogany and oak, with a black walnut border. The grand staircase, as well as the wainscoting following its ascent, is also of oak and mahogany, and its landing, designed for the small orchestras that once played on it, has three large windows of clear, frosted, and stained glass. The living room, which houses a library, and the den, where guests may watch color television, both have ornate tiled fireplaces. All the guest rooms are furnished in antiques.

Accommodations: 7 rooms with private bath. *Smoking:* Not permitted in public rooms. *Children:* Permitted. *Pets:* Permitted. *Driving Instructions:* Bread and Roses is in the center of town, one block from Fort Anne and two from the post office.

Camelot

Box 31, Musquodoboit Harbor, Nova Scotia, Canada BOJ 2LO. (902) 889-2198. *Hostess:* Mrs. P. M. Holgate (Charlie).

This large 1858 farmhouse has 110 hemlock trees in its front yard and a backyard salmon pool. Charlie's 4.5 acres are tucked away in the bend of a river. The property abounds with racoons, foxes, porcupines, minks, and "otter" kinds of animals. All the guest rooms overlook the meandering river which in summer is warm enough for swimming.

Charlie said an antique mahogany table, which extends to 22 feet, is the "catalyst of my operation," an international site for making friends. But a moment later she claimed it was her marble fireplace that brought her and her guests together.

When the river swells and turns into rapids, guests frequently go white-water canoeing or kayaking. Swimming is best during the three hours of low tide.

Accommodations: 5 rooms with shared bath. *Smoking:* Permitted downstairs only. *Children:* Permitted. *Pets:* Permitted if well behaved. *Driving Instructions:* Camelot is 30 miles east of Halifax on Route 7 East.

Beaver Valley. Glenelg is a renovated 1888 lakeside schoolhouse shaded by mature maple trees. Its four guest rooms have their original metal ceilings, which are embellished with sinuous curlicues. The location is convenient to the Bear Valley Ski Area, and being on a lake, couldn't be closer to fishing and canoeing. *Represented by:* Country Host, (519) 941-7633. $25–$35.

Caledon. Situated on 3 acres near Caledon, Lothlorien is a restored Victorian farmhouse. A spiral staircase leads to the guest rooms. Hosts Gord and Joan are interested in cooking and their two Irish setters, among other things. Their house is close to cross-country and downhill skiing facilities, and the Bruce Trail is nearby. *Represented by:* Country Host, (519) 941-7633. $25–$35.

Caledon East. Billie completely modernized and decorated this turn-of-the-century home; she herself lives in the log cabin next door. The upstairs bedrooms overlook the pool or the garden, and the ground floor of the house features exposed beams, walls covered with barn boards, and a fireplace. Billie is more than pleased to come over to the house and cook her guests' breakfasts whenever they happen to be ready for it. *Represented by:* Country Host, (519) 941-7633. $25–$35.

Collingwood. Bob and Joan's large home, NottNottowa, is situated on 20 acres, which include an orchard. The house is close to the Blue Mountain resorts. Bob and Joan, who offer two rooms to guests and welcome children, know a great deal about the area (a lovely one) and enjoy sharing what they know with guests. *Represented by:* Country Host, (519) 941-7633. $25–$35.

Devil's Glen. Jokingly named Seldom Rest is a working farm, which should, perhaps, have been named Often Entertain. Ruby's cooking is famous throughout the district, which is a mecca for hikers, skiers, and fans of Georgian Bay watchers. *Represented by:* Country Host, (519) 941-7633. $25–$35.

Hockley Valley. Paul and Ingrid have a bungalow on 2 acres of grounds not far from scenic Hockley Valley, which is popular among bird-watchers and photographers. First-rate trout fishing is less than a mile away, and golf is also close by. Paul and Ingrid offer guests two double rooms. *Represented by:* Country Host, (519) 941-7633. $25–$35.

Mono Mills. A spacious home on 2 acres of green rolling hills, this guest house has a view of Toronto's CN Tower, which is 40 miles away. Summer and winter activities (fishing and golf, skiing and ice-skating) are nearby. *Represented by:* Country Host, (519) 941-7633. $25–$35.

Orangeville. The garden of this split-level home opens onto the Minora Conservation area, an all-season recreation area with both a beach and cross-country ski trails. Nearby Orangeville Raceway will appeal to racing fans, as well as anyone who enjoys a first-rate buffet. *Represented by:* Country Host, (519) 941-7633. $25–$35.

Shelburne. This restored 1909 house is situated on a 116-acre farm that has both donkeys and ponies. Fond of children, hosts Hilda and Cecil frequently take them for donkey, pony, or hay rides. The area offers excellent fishing and hiking, and Wasaga Beach, on Georgian Bay, is only 20 miles distant. *Represented by:* Country Host, (519) 941-7633. $25–$35.

Eglinton and Kipling. This accommodation, located at the highest point in Toronto, commands a unique view of the city. It is in a condominium apartment with a carpeted terrace, air conditioning, a heated pool, a sauna, a gym room, laundry facilities, and security parking—all for the use of guests. Call Beaven, (416) 248-5722. Member of Toronto Bed & Breakfast, (416) 769-0612 (evenings and weekends only). $30–$40.

Queen and Greenwood. Your hosts, who speak German and some Slavic languages, as well as English, have three guest rooms available. They live in a detached home in Toronto's beach area, within walking distance of Lake Ontario and 15 minutes via streetcar from downtown Toronto. Call Arsovsky, (416) 465-2411. Member of Toronto Bed & Breakfast, (416) 769-0612 (evenings and weekends only). $30–$40.

Don Valley and Sheppard. A bedroom with a double bed in a large condominium apartment, this accommodation includes two bathrooms, air conditioning, color television, and many antiques. There are no restrictions as to smoking or drinking, but bring your own. The building is 25 minutes from downtown Toronto. Call Connell, (416) 491-5242. Member of Toronto Bed & Breakfast, (416) 769-0612 (evenings and weekends only). $25–$35.

Danforth and Main. This ninety-year old, antique-filled house has three guest rooms, one of them with a queen-size brass bed. Near Taylor Park and Toronto's Greek section, this guest house is 20 minutes from downtown. Call Fox, (416) 690-5549. Member of Toronto Bed & Breakfast, (416) 769-0612 (evenings and weekends only). $33–$40.

Bathurst and College. In the Kensington area, which is convenient to all of downtown Toronto's attractions, this accommodation consists of three rooms available to guests. One—a large master bedroom with air conditioning and television—has a balcony overlooking the street. Guests are invited to use the backyard's table and barbecue. English, Ukrainian, Polish, and German are spoken. "Come sample our blueberry muffins." Call Martyniuk, (416) 364-7726. Member of Toronto Bed & Breakfast, (416) 769-0612 (evenings and weekends only). $25–$35.

Sheppard and Don Mills. The Pattersons, who invite you to use their large outdoor swimming pool, serve a full breakfast in the sun room beside the pool. The house is ten minutes from the Ontario Science Center and 20 minutes from downtown. French and English are spoken. Call Patterson, (416) 493-3135. Member of Toronto Bed & Breakfast, (416) 769-0612 (evenings and weekends only). $25–$35.

Bloor and Runnymede. The founders of the Toronto Bed and Breakfast agency, the Lees live in a three-bedroom, two-bathroom semidetached house in Toronto's west end. They have one room for guests. The house is 20 minutes from downtown and within walking distance of High Park and the many shops on the Bloor West Village Strip. Call Lee, (416) 769-0612 (evenings and weekends only). $25–$35.

University and Dundas. These two guest accommodations, one a single room and the other a double, are in an 1882 Victorian row house in the heart of Toronto that overlooks Grange Park. The Art Gallery of Ontario, Kensington Market, and the University of Toronto are a short walk away. Your hosts, who welcome adult guests only, have two Dalmatians and three cats. Call By the Gallery, (416) 368-4470. Member of Toronto Bed & Breakfast, (416) 769-0612 (evenings and weekends only). $30–$40.

College and Spadina. These two guest accommodations are in a turn-of-the-century home in the heart of Toronto. Both rooms, one double and one single, have comforters on the beds. Your hosts, who have two small daughters, shop daily at Kensington Market, and they will, on request, prepare gourmet brunches, picnics, or dinners. Call Hertzog, (416) 598-4063. Member of Toronto Bed & Breakfast, (416) 769-0612 (evenings and weekends only). $30–$40.

Don Mills and Shepard. Your hosts invite guests to sun in their garden, watch television in their family room, and join them for a cup of tea each evening. These accommodations, twenty minutes from downtown, consist of two rooms for guests. English, French, and Spanish are spoken. Call Maher, (416) 494-5433. Member of Toronto Bed & Breakfast, (416) 769-0612 (evenings and weekends only). $25–$38.

Eight-Room Duplex. This accommodation—either of two rooms in an eight-room lower duplex—comes complete with eggs Benedict for breakfast. Your hosts, a recently retired couple fluent in English and French, make silver jewelry as a hobby. Convenient to public transportation. *Represented by:* Montreal Bed & Breakfast, (514) 735-7493. $25–$40.

Stained-Glass Windows. Your hostess, who enjoys and teaches bridge, offers two single and one double bedroom to guests. The home, convenient to the subway in the northeastern section of town, features stained-glass windows and oak doors and trim. *Represented by:* Montreal Bed & Breakfast, (514) 735-7493. $25–$40.

Fireplace. This accommodation offers one single and one twin-bedded room for guests. The living room, accented with oak, has a fireplace. In the northeastern section of Notre Dame de Grace, this six-room semidetached home is two minutes from a subway direct to downtown Montreal. *Represented by:* Montreal Bed & Breakfast, (514) 735-7493. $25–$40.

Cottage. A nine-room semidetached cottage in the Notre Dame de Grace section of Montreal, this accommodation offers one double- and one twin-bedded guest room. Your hostess plays with the Montreal Symphony, and two dogs and a cat play with whoever encourages them. *Represented by:* Montreal Bed & Breakfast, (514) 735-7493. $25–$40.

Outremont. This ten-room cottage in the old and elegant section of Outremont has been in the same family for seventy-five years. It is near several of Montreal's prettier parks and the chic Lourier Avenue. Two guest rooms have double beds, and one has twins. There is excellent transportation to downtown. *Represented by:* Montreal Bed & Breakfast, (514) 735-7493. $25–$40.

Nine-Room Duplex. Your bilingual hosts offer guests a large master bedroom with a full private bath. This nine-room lower duplex is in the old Outremont section, and your hosts enjoy showing guests around town. *Represented by:* Montreal Bed & Breakfast, (514) 735-7493. $25–$40.

Beaconsfield. Overlooking Lake St. Louis, this nine-room cottage has three rooms available to guests—two singles and a twin. The location, twenty minutes by car from downtown, is in the West Island community of Beaconsfield. The household includes two cats and a dog. *Represented by:* Montreal Bed & Breakfast, (514) 735-7493. $25–$40.

INDEX WITH RATES AND CREDIT INFORMATION

These rates reflect the cost per day of a single and a double room; if one rate is given, it represents the cost of double-occupancy accommodations. The rates are subject to change, and some vary according to season.

Credit-card abbreviations:
AE: American Express
D: Diners Club
MC: MasterCard
V: Visa
NCC: No credit cards accepted

THE COMPLEAT TRAVELER'S READER REPORT

To: *The Compleat Traveler*
c/o Burt Franklin & Co., Inc.
235 East 44th Street
New York, New York 10017 U.S.A.

Dear Compleat Traveler:

I have used your *Great American Guest House Book.* I would like to offer the following ☐ new recommendation, ☐ comment, ☐ suggestion, ☐ criticism, ☐ or complaint about:

Name of Guest House/Bed & Breakfast

____

Referral service used: ____________________________

Address: __________________________________

____

Comments:

Date of my visit: ______________ Length of stay: ____________

From (name): _______________________________

Address ___________________________________

____________________ Telephone: ___________________